Democracy and Race

THE ASIAN AMERICAN EXPERIENCE

Democracy and Race

ASIAN AMERICANS AND WORLD WAR II

Ronald Takaki

PROFESSOR OF ETHNIC STUDIES
THE UNIVERSITY OF CALIFORNIA AT BERKELEY

Adapted by Rebecca Stefoff

WITH CAROL TAKAKI

Chelsea House Publishers

New York ✳ *Philadelphia*

Chelsea House Publishers

EDITORIAL DIRECTOR   Richard Rennert
EXECUTIVE MANAGING EDITOR   Karyn Gullen Browne
COPY CHIEF   Robin James
PICTURE EDITOR   Adrian G. Allen
ART DIRECTOR   Robert Mitchell
MANUFACTURING DIRECTOR   Gerald Levine

The Asian American Experience

SENIOR EDITOR   Jake Goldberg
SERIES DESIGN   Marjorie Zaum

Staff for *Democracy and Race*
EDITORIAL ASSISTANT   Kelsey Goss
PICTURE RESEARCHER   Sandy Jones

Adapted and reprinted from *Strangers from a Different Shore,*
© 1989 by Ronald Takaki, by arrangement with the author and
Little, Brown and Company, Inc.

First Printing

1   3   5   7   9   8   6   4   2

Library of Congress Cataloging-in-Publication Data
Takaki, Ronald T., 1939–

   Democracy and Race: Asian Americans and World War II / Ronald
Takaki.
      p. cm.—(The Asian American experience)
   Includes bibliographical references and index.
ISBN 0-7910-2184–X
   I. World War, 1939-1945-Asian Americans and the war. 2. Asian
Americans-History-20th Century. 3. United States-Ethnic relations.
            I. Title. II. Series: Asian American experience (New York,
N.Y.)

      D753.7.T35 1994   94–6175
      940.53'150395073-dc20   CIP

Contents

Fearful and confused, a young Japanese American girl sits amid her family's belongings, awaiting "evacuation" to an American concentration camp at the beginning of World War II.

AS A CHILD IN HAWAII, I GREW UP IN A MULTICULTURAL corner of America. My own family had roots in Japan and China.

Grandfather Kasuke Okawa arrived in Hawaii in 1866, and my father, Toshio Takaki, came as a 13-year-old boy in 1918. My stepfather, Koon Keu Young, sailed from China to the islands when he was a teenager.

My neighbors were Japanese, Chinese, Hawaiian, Filipino, Portuguese, and Korean. Behind my house, Alice Liu and her friends played the traditional Chinese game of mahjongg late into the night, the clicking of the tiles lulling me to sleep.

Next to us the Miuras flew billowing and colorful carp kites on Japanese boy's day. I heard voices with different accents, different languages, and saw children of different colors.

Together we went barefoot to school and played games like baseball and *jan ken po*. We spoke "pidgin English," a melodious language of the streets and community. "Hey, da kind tako ono, you know," we would say, combining English, Japanese, and Hawaiian. "This octopus is delicious." Racially and culturally diverse, we all thought of ourselves as Americans.

But we did not know why families representing such an array of nationalities from different shores were living together and sharing their cultures and a common language. Our teachers and textbooks did not explain the diversity of our community or the sources of our unity.

After graduation from high school, I attended a college in a midwestern town where I found myself invited to "dinners for foreign students" sponsored by local churches and clubs like the Rotary. I politely tried to explain to my kind hosts that I was not a "foreign student." My fellow students and even my professors would ask me how long I had been in America and where I had learned to speak English. "In this country," I would reply. And sometimes I would add: "I was born in America, and my family has been here for three generations."

Asian Americans have been here for over 150 years. They are diverse, coming originally from countries such as China, Japan, Korea, the Philippines, India, Vietnam, Laos, and Cambodia. Many of them live in Chinatowns, the colorful streets filled with sidewalk vegetable stands and crowds of people carrying shopping bags; their communities are also called Little Tokyo, Koreatown, and Little Saigon. Asian Americans work in hot kitchens and bus tables in restaurants with elegant names like Jade Pagoda and Bombay Spice. In garment factories, Chinese and Korean women hunch over whirling sewing machines, their babies sleeping nearby on blankets. In the Silicon Valley of California, rows and rows of Vietnamese and Laotian women serve as the eyes and hands of production assembly lines for computer chip industries. Tough Chinese gang members strut on Grant Avenue in San Francisco and Canal Street in New York's Chinatown. In La Crosse, Wisconsin, Hmong refugees from Laos, now dependent on welfare, sit and stare at the snowdrifts outside their windows. Asian American engineers do complex research in the laboratories of the high-technology industries along

Route 128 in Massachusetts. Asian Americans seem to be everywhere on university campuses.

Today, Asian Americans belong to the fastest growing ethnic group in the United States. Kept out of the United States by immigration restriction laws in the 19th and early 20th centuries, Asians have recently been coming again to America. The 1965 immigration act reopened the gates to immigrants from Asia, allowing 20,000 immigrants from each country to enter every year. In the early 1990s, half of all immigrants entering annually are Asian.

The growth of the Asian American population has been dramatic: In 1960, there were only 877,934 Asians in the United States, representing a mere one half of 1% of the American people. Thirty years later, they numbered about seven million, or 3% of the population. They included 1,645,000 Chinese, 1,400,000 Filipinos, 845,000 Japanese, 815,000 Asian Indians, 800,000 Koreans, 614,000 Vietnamese, 150,000 Laotians, 147,000 Cambodians, and 90,000 Hmong. By the year 2000, Asian Americans will probably represent 4% of the total United States population. In California, Asian Americans already make up 10% of the state's inhabitants, compared with 7.5% for African Americans.

Yet very little is known about Asian Americans and their history. Many existing history books give Asian Americans only passing notice—or overlook them entirely. "When one hears Americans tell of the immigrants who built this nation," Congressman Norman Mineta of California observed, "one is often led to believe that all our forebearers came from Europe. When one hears stories about the pioneers going West to shape the land, the Asian immigrant is rarely mentioned."

Indeed, many history books have equated "American" with "white" or "European" in origin. In his prize-winning study, *The Uprooted*, Harvard historian Oscar Handlin presented—to use the book's subtitle—"the Epic Story of the Great Migrations that Made the American People." But Handlin's "epic story" completely left out the "uprooted" from lands across the Pacific Ocean and the "great migrations" from Asia that also helped to make "the American people." As Americans, we have origins in Europe, the Americas, Africa, and also Asia.

We need to include Asians in the history of America. How and why, we ask in this series, were the experiences of these various groups—Chinese, Japanese, Korean, Filipino, Asian Indian, and Southeast Asian—similar to and different from each other? Comparing the experiences of different nationalities can help us see what events were particular to a group and also highlight the experiences they all shared.

Why did Asian immigrants leave everything they knew and loved to come to a strange world so far away? They were "pushed" by hardships in the homelands and "pulled" by demands for their labor in Canada, Brazil, and especially the United States. But what were their own fierce dreams— from the first enterprising Chinese miners of the 1850s in search of "Gold Mountain" to the recent refugees fleeing frantically on helicopters and leaking boats from the ravages of war in Vietnam?

Besides their points of origin, we need to examine the experiences of Asian Americans in different geographical regions, especially Hawaii compared with the mainland. The time of arrival also shaped their lives and communities. About one million people entered the United States between the California gold rush of 1849 and the 1924 immigration act that cut off the flow of peoples from Asian countries. After a break of some 40 years, a second group numbering about four million came between 1965 and 1990. How do we compare the two waves of Asian immigration?

To answer our questions in these volumes, we must study Asian Americans as men and women with minds, wills, and voices. By "voices" we mean their own words and stories as told in their oral histories, conversations, speeches, and songs as well as their own writings—diaries, letters, newspapers, novels, and poems. We need to know the ordinary people.

So much of history has been the story of kings and elites, as if the "little people" were invisible and voiceless. An Asian American told an interviewer: "I am a second-generation Korean American without any achievements in life and I have no education. What is it you want to hear from me? My life is not worth telling to anyone." Similarly, a Chinese immigrant said: "You know, it seems to me there's no use in me telling you all this! I was just a simple worker, a farm worker around here. My story is not going to interest anybody." But others realize they are worthy of attention. "What is it you want to know?" an old Filipino immigrant asked a researcher. "Talk about history. What's that . . . ah, the story of my life . . . and how people lived with each other in my time."

Their stories can enable us to understand Asians as actors in the making of history and as people entitled to dignity. "I hope this survey do a lot of good for Chinese people," a Chinese man told an interviewer from Stanford University in the 1920s. "Make American people realize that Chinese people are humans. I think very few American people really know anything about Chinese." Elderly Asians want the younger generations to know about their experiences. "Our stories should be listened to by many young people," said a 91-year-old retired Japanese plantation laborer. "It's for their sake. We really had a hard time, you know."

The stories of Asian immigrations belong to our country's history. They need to be recorded in our history books, for they reflect the making of America as a nation of immigrants, as a place where men and women came to find a new beginning. At first, many Asian immigrants—probably most of them—saw themselves as sojourners, or temporary migrants. Like many European immigrants such as the Italians and Greeks, they came to America thinking they would be here only a short time. They had left their wives and children behind in their homelands. Their plan was to work here for a few years and then return home with money. But, after their arrival, many found themselves staying. They became settlers instead of remaining sojourners. Bringing their families to their adopted country, they began putting down new roots in America.

But, coming here from Asia, many of America's immigrants found they were not allowed to feel at home in the United States. Even their grandchildren and great-grandchildren still find they are not viewed and accepted as Americans. "We feel that we're a guest in someone else's house," said third generation Ron Wakabayashi, National Director of the Japanese American Citizens League, "that we can never really relax and put our feet on the table."

Behind Wakabayashi's complaint is the question: Why have Asian Americans been considered outsiders? America's immigrants from Pacific shores found they were forced to remain strangers in the new land. Their experiences here were profoundly different from the experiences of European immigrants. Asian immigrants had qualities they could not change or hide—the shape of their eyes, the color of their hair, the complexion of their skin. They were subjected not only to cultural and ethnic prejudice but also to racism. Unlike the Irish and other groups from Europe, Asian immigrants were not treated as individuals but as members of a group with distinctive physical characteristics. Regardless of their personal merits, they sadly discovered, they could not gain acceptance in the larger society.

Unlike European immigrants, Asians were victimized by laws and policies that discriminated on the basis of race. The Chinese Exclusion Act of 1882 barred the Chinese from coming to America because they were Chinese. The National Origins Act of 1924 totally prohibited Japanese immigration.

The laws determined not only who could come to America but also who could become citizens. Decades before Asian immigration began, the United States had already defined the complexion of its citizens: the Naturalization Law of 1790 had specified that naturalized citizenship was to be reserved for "whites." This law remained in effect until 1952. Unlike white ethnic immigrants from countries like Ireland, Asian immigrants were denied citizenship and also the right to vote.

But America also had an opposing tradition and vision, springing from the reality of racial and cultural "diversity." Ours has been, as Walt Whitman celebrated so lyrically, "a teeming Nation of nations" composed of a "vast, surging, hopeful army of workers," a new society where all should be welcomed, "Chinese, Irish, German,—all, all, without exceptions." In the early 20th century, a Japanese immigrant described in poetry a lesson that had been learned by farm laborers of different nationalities—Japanese, Filipino, Mexican, and Asian Indian:

> *People harvesting*
> *Work together unaware*
> *Of racial problems.*

A Filipino immigrant laborer in California expressed a similar hope and understanding. America was, Macario Bulosan told his brother Carlos, "not a land of one race or one class of men" but "a new world" of respect and unconditional opportunities for all who toiled and suffered from oppression, from "the first Indian that offered peace in Manhattan to the last Filipino pea pickers." Asian immigrants came here, as one of them expressed it, searching for "a door into America" and seeking "to build a new life with untried materials." He asked: "Would it be possible for an immigrant like me to become a part of the American dream?"

This series invites students to learn how Asian Americans belong to the larger story of the rich multicultural mosaic called the United States of America.

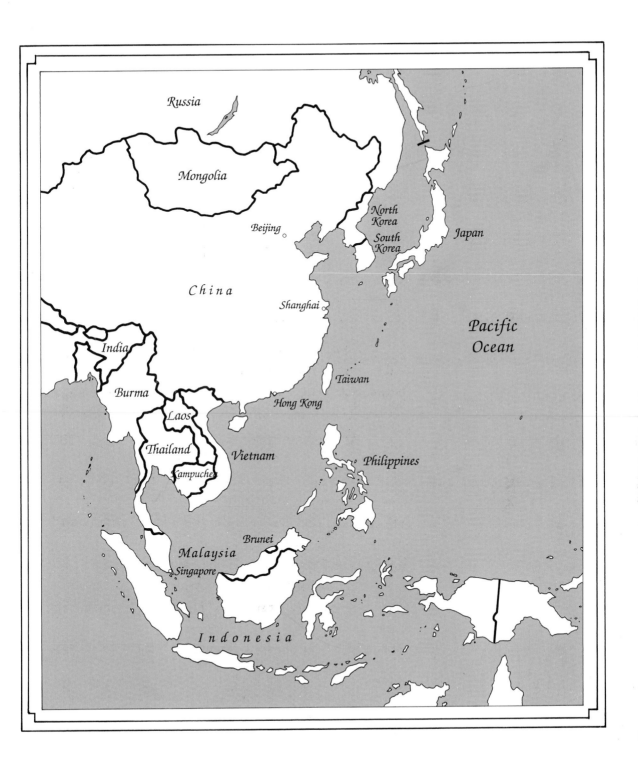

Japanese troops celebrate their capture of Bataan in the Philippine Islands. The war that engulfed the Pacific brought changes to the lives of many Asian Americans.

ONE SUNDAY AFTERNOON IN DECEMBER OF 1941, A FILI-
pino man named Carlos Bulosan was sitting in a bar in Los
Angeles. He was thinking about his life: about his childhood
in the Philippine Islands and about the ten years he had spent
in the United States. As a child, Bulosan had dreamed of
America as a land of hope and freedom. But as a man, he had
found the dream hard to reach. The United States, the land
of opportunity, was also a place where immigrants like Bulosan often met hardship and prejudice. Sometimes Bulosan
feared that he would never be accepted as an American. He
felt like "an exile in America."

All at once Bulosan's thoughts were broken by a
blaring newsbreak on the radio. "Japan bombs Pearl Harbor!"
the announcer cried. Like all Americans in that historic
moment, Bulosan felt as if his world had suddenly turned
upside down. He rushed outside, trembling and looking for a
familiar face. "It has come, Carlos!" his brother Macario
shouted. The two brothers walked aimlessly in the streets,
stunned by the news. War had been raging in Asia and the
Pacific for some time, but the United States had not joined
the conflict. Now, however, Japan had bombed an American
naval base in Hawaii. Surely the United States would enter
the war. What would this war mean for Bulosan's mother and
sisters in the Philippines? And what would it mean for all the
Asian people in America?

A few months later, Macario Bulosan joined the army.
As he watched his brother ride away on the army bus, Carlos
Bulosan realized that the war would change Macario. It would
change everyone, all of American society. "If I met him again,
I would not be the same," Carlos thought. "He would not be

the same, either. Our world was this one, but a new one was being born."

Bulosan knew that the war would be a crucial dividing line in the history of Filipinos and other Asians in America. The war came crashing down on Asian American communities from Hawaii to New York City. Large international forces were pulling Filipinos, Koreans, Asian Indians, Chinese, and Japanese into a whirlpool of chaos and change. The war would give immigrants and their American-born children a new reason to think about their identities as Asians and as Americans. For years, Asians had been denied full equality in the United States. Laws kept them from becoming U.S. citizens, from owning land, from marrying whites. Asians had been treated as aliens, as "strangers from a different shore." Now they would be asked to support their country in crisis, to serve in the U.S. armed forces.

The war would also challenge America's image of itself as a democracy. The United States would have to recognize its own ethnic diversity. Americans would be asked to overcome racial prejudice, to extend their democratic ideals to immigrants of color. They would be called upon to give a new answer to the question "Who is an American?"

The war that the United States joined after the attack on Pearl Harbor is known as World War II. It truly was a *world* war, touching almost every place on earth. Most of the fighting, however, took place in Europe and in eastern Asia and the Pacific Ocean.

War broke out in Europe in 1939, when Germany, under the leadership of Adolf Hitler and the Nazi party, invaded Poland. Several decades of peace talks and attempts

to avoid war had failed, and Germany was bent on expanding its territory. Great Britain and France, known as the Allied powers, joined forces against Germany and Italy, who were called the Axis powers. Later Russia (then known as the Soviet Union) joined the Allies, as did many other countries. Other nations joined the Axis, too. Before the war was over, 57 nations fought on one side or the other.

After seizing Poland, Germany went on to invade a string of European countries, including Denmark, the Netherlands, Belgium, France, Greece, and Yugoslavia. German forces successfully occupied many countries but failed to achieve other goals. Most of France, for example, fell under German control, but Great Britain was never invaded, and the German invasion of Russia was driven back by Russian troops.

The United States was deeply divided over the question of whether or not to join the war. Some Americans, seeing the plight of the Poles, French, and other European peoples

American warships in flames after the surprise attack on Pearl Harbor, Hawaii.

whose countries were being overrun by the German army, felt that the United States should enter the war against Germany. In addition, many Americans opposed the Nazi philosophy, which included ideas about racial and ethnic superiority. Americans and others who believed in democracy were repelled by the Nazi notion that white people of European descent, especially those of "pure" Nordic or German blood, were better than other kinds of people. Tragically, this belief in Nordic racial superiority led to such horrors as the Holocaust, in which the German government slaughtered millions of Jews and other ethnic and religious minorities.

Hickam airfield during the Japanese attack on December 7, 1941. Outrage over the attack brought the United States into World War II.

At first, however, the majority of Americans did not want to rush headlong into a foreign war. The United States had not been attacked or invaded, and families across the land still grieved for the hundreds of thousands of American soldiers who had been killed and wounded in the last great European conflict, World War I (1914–18). In the first year or so of the war, most Americans believed that the United States should send aid to Great Britain and other embattled allies but should not enter the fight.

On the other side of the world, war was building in Asia and the Pacific years before the fighting began in Europe. Japan had entered a period of rapid change and modernization in the late 1860s. Within a few years, the Japanese countryside was dotted with Western-style factories and schools. After centuries of isolation from other nations, Japan now found itself part of the international community. Japan's military leaders, a powerful group within the government, wanted their country to become a world power. They began strengthening Japan's armed forces. By the end of the 19th century, Japan was a formidable military presence in Asia.

Japan invaded the neighboring country of Korea in 1904. Six years later, Japan annexed Korea—that is, formally claimed it as Japanese territory. In 1931, Japan seized control of part of Manchuria, a region in northeastern China. In the years that followed, Japanese forces moved into many parts of China, and in 1937 full-scale war broke out between Chinese troops and the invading Japanese. Japan had expected to conquer China swiftly, but the Chinese put up a determined resistance, and the war dragged on for years.

In 1940, Japan became one of the Axis powers by signing a pact with Germany and Italy. Although the United

States began sending supplies to the Chinese defense forces in the spring of 1941, it did not become directly involved in the war. Throughout that year, Americans remained reluctant to be drawn into the fighting in either Europe or Asia.

The mood of the United States changed instantly when Pearl Harbor was bombed. Suddenly the conflict was no longer a foreign war—bombs had been dropped on U.S. soil, and Americans had been killed. The Japanese were now enemies of the United States. Americans contemptuously called them "Japs" and vowed to fight back. On December 8, 1941, the day after the Japanese attack on Hawaii, the U.S. Congress and President Franklin D. Roosevelt declared war on Japan. A short time later the United States also entered the war in Europe against Germany and Italy, Japan's Axis partners.

The entry of the United States into World War II tilted the balance of power in favor of the Allies, but the war was not won easily or quickly. Bitter air, sea, and land fighting dragged on until 1945, when Allied armies encircled Berlin, the capital of Germany, and forced Germany to surrender in May. Japan continued to fight until August, when U.S. planes dropped the only atomic bombs that have ever been used in war on the Japanese cities of Hiroshima and Nagasaki. Faced with destruction unlike any that had been known before, Japan surrendered. The war was finally over.

Carlos Bulosan had foreseen that the war would affect all parts of American society. Certainly the war had a deep and long-lasting impact on the lives of Bulosan's fellow Asian Americans. People from Asia had been coming to Hawaii and the U.S. mainland since the middle of the 19th century. They came in search of work and a better life, first from China, then

from Japan, Korea, the Philippines, and India. The immigrants found work on the sugar plantations of Hawaii and in the gold mines and railroad camps of the American West. They worked as farm laborers, planting and harvesting the crops that built America's agricultural industry; and they opened stores and businesses and built communities, hoping to make a place for themselves in the American landscape. All too often, though, they were greeted with prejudice and scorn.

    As temporary laborers, Asian immigrants were welcome—but in the eyes of many white Americans, they were not welcome as permanent settlers. Starting in the late 19th century, laws limited the number of Asian immigrants who

Hawaiian residents watch the Japanese aircraft attack. The bombing of Pearl Harbor caused communities in Hawaii and on the U.S. mainland to examine the place of Japanese immigrants in American society.

could enter the United States, and in 1924, the federal government passed an immigration act that ended all immigration from Asia. Asians who were already in the United States were allowed to stay, but they could not become citizens, which meant that they could not vote or hold public office. However, their children born in America automatically became U.S. citizens.

The Asian Americans experienced World War II both as Americans and as Asians. Having made America their home, they shared the fear, sorrow, and patriotic pride felt by all Americans in wartime. Many young Asian American men fought in the war, side by side with black and white soldiers, and many were killed. Asian Americans felt a special grief and

*President Franklin D.
Roosevelt signs the
declaration that put
the United States at
war with Japan.*

24

anger, however, when they listened to news of the war in Asia and knew that their ancestral homelands were being ravaged. Americans of Japanese descent found the war years most difficult, for they were treated as enemies, even though the majority of them had been born and raised in the United States. Other Asians in the United States sometimes suffered the penalty of being mistaken for Japanese and treated with suspicion and hostility.

The war brought some positive changes as well. It created job opportunities for some Asian Americans, and it also opened the door to citizenship for some. Above all, the war ushered in changes in the way Americans looked at themselves and their society. By the end of the war, people in the United States were realizing that a democratic nation could no longer practice racial discrimination. People of color were Americans, too, and they deserved equal treatment. Progress toward equality would be slow and unsteady, but the move toward a multicultural America was under way.

Filipino scouts man an antiaircraft gun. During the war, the soldiers
of the Philippines joined forces with American troops.

Chapter Two

"On to Bataan"

ONE FILIPINO WOMAN NEVER FORGOT THE JAPANESE attack on Pearl Harbor. The Japanese planes swooped down on December 7, 1941, shattering the calm of this Sunday morning in Hawaii. "The airplanes looked like toys but they were shooting and dropping bombs on us," recalled Apolinaria Gusman Oclaray, who had left the Philippines with her husband in 1928. "I thought it was play, you know practice, and I asked my husband, 'How come the airplanes are firing?' And he said, 'Because this is a real war and a real war is like that.'"

Seven hours after the attack on Pearl Harbor, Japanese forces invaded the Philippine Islands, a U.S. territory. The Philippines became the scene of some of the most bitter and important battles fought in the Pacific during World War II. On the Bataan peninsula of Luzon Island, the Japanese invaders met spirited resistance from American and Filipino troops.

Four long months later, on April 9, 1942, a news correspondent described the fall of Bataan: "The gallant United States and Philippine forces in Bataan peninsula surrendered today after enduring the tortures of hell. . . . They were beaten, but it was a fight that ought to make every American bow his head in tribute. . . . The Americans fought for everything they loved, as did the Filipinos, WITH THEIR FIERCE LOVE OF LIBERTY."

In her tribute to the brave men of Bataan, Eleanor Roosevelt, the wife of President Roosevelt, spoke of the interracial brotherhood forged on the bloodstained battlefield. She said, "Fighting in Bataan has been an excellent example of what happens when two different races respect each other. Men of different races and backgrounds have fought side by side and praised each other's heroism and courage."

Carlos Bulosan conveyed in poetry the meaning of Bataan for Filipinos:

> *Bataan has fallen.*
> *With heads bloody but unbowed, we yielded to the*
> * enemy. . . .*
> *We have stood up uncomplaining.*
> *Besieged on land and blockaded by sea,*
> *We have done all that human endurance could*
> * bear. . . .*
> *Our defeat is our victory.*

At Bataan thousands of Filipinos had fought beside American soldiers. Stories of Filipino bravery forced white people in the United States to view Filipino immigrants more respectfully. Suddenly there was something "in the air," Filipino writer Manuel Buaken noticed, that said America had learned to respect Filipinos. "No longer on the streetcar do I feel myself in the presence of my enemies," he said. "We Filipinos are the same—it is Americans that have changed in their recognition of us." A Filipino man who worked in a railroad car was pleasantly surprised by the sudden change in the way white travelers treated him. "I am very much embarrassed," he remarked. "They treat me as if I have just arrived from Bataan."

Meanwhile, Filipinos in America worried about the Philippines and the loved ones they had left there. They wanted to defend their homeland, and they immediately rushed to the recruiting offices to volunteer for the armed forces. They were turned away, however. The Filipino immi-

grants were classified as "nationals," not U.S. citizens, which meant that they could not serve in the military.

Filipinos in the United States were frustrated and angry because they could not join the war. When Carlos Bulosan learned that his village of Binalonan had been crushed by Japanese tanks racing toward Manila, the capital of the Philippines, he went to the nearest recruiting office, hoping to sign up. Later he said, "As I stood in line waiting for my turn, I thought of a one-legged American Revolutionary patriot of whom I had read. But Filipinos were not being accepted."

They had to get into this war, Filipinos insisted. President Roosevelt listened to their pleas and promptly changed the draft law so that Filipinos could join the armed forces. On February 19, 1942, the secretary of war announced that the First Filipino Infantry Regiment was being formed. "This new unit is formed in recognition of the intense loyalty and patriotism of those Filipinos who are now residing in the

Everyone took part in the war effort in the Philippines. Members of the Women's Auxiliary Service were trained to help with Red Cross work.

29

United States," he said. "It provides for them a means of serving in the armed forces of the United States, and the eventual opportunity of fighting on the soil of their homeland."

Filipinos eagerly responded to the call to arms. In California alone, 16,000 men—two-fifths of the state's Filipino population—registered to enter the military. More than 7,000 Filipinos served in two Filipino infantry regiments. "Their enthusiasm and discipline are far superior to any I have seen in my army career," declared their white commander. "The minute you put one of these boys in uniform he wants a rifle. The minute he gets a rifle he wants to get on a boat. He can't understand why we don't ship him out right away, so he can start [fighting]."

The *American Legion Magazine* called the war "a personal grudge" for the Filipino American soldiers. As one of these soldiers said, they had "a personal reason to be training to fight the invaders." They wanted to defend the Philippines. "My home and my family and all the things that were dear to me as a boy," explained Doroteo Vite in 1942, "are there in the path of the Japanese war machine." Another said that he met white men who were "thrilled" at the sight of Filipinos in America, admiring them as representatives of the people of the Philippines, who were putting up a fierce fight against the Japanese.

Filipinos in the United States were eager to get back to the Philippines to fight for the liberation of their homeland, which had fallen to Japan by May of 1942. The regimental song of the First Filipino Infantry Regiment was "On to Bataan." Shipped to the Pacific for duty, the soldiers were anxious for action. "After we came from Australia by submarine we went to the Philippines," recalled one man. "We trained in Australia under General MacArthur . . . learned how to roll parachutes, jump in combat . . . how to kill people noiselessly." Filipino soldiers made unique and valuable contributions to the war in the Pacific. They operated behind enemy lines, carrying out sabotage missions to destroy Japanese communications. They also served as spies, gathering vital information. A U.S. lieutenant general reported that the information gathered by Filipino soldiers was "of the greatest assistance to impending military operations." He added, "By their loyalty, daring, and skillful performance of duty under hazardous conditions, they materially accelerated the campaign for the recapture of the Philippine Islands."

Many Filipino American soldiers also saw the war as a chance to fight for their freedom at home in the United

A Filipino veteran of the Bataan campaign laughs at a Japanese propaganda poster. The Filipinos dogged defense of Bataan earned high praise from the American troops who fought side by side with them.

States. The fact that they could wear a soldier's uniform was a political statement. "In a few months I will be wearing Uncle Sam's olive-drab army uniform," said a Filipino. "I am looking forward to that day, not with misgiving but with a boyish anticipation of doing something which up to now I have never been allowed to do—serving as an equal with American boys." The wife of a Filipino soldier claimed that the war gave Filipinos the chance to show themselves to America as "soldiers of democracy," as "men, not houseboys."

To Filipinos, joining the army gave them membership in American society. "In all the years I was here before the United States went into the war," a Filipino soldier observed, "I felt that I did not belong here. I was a stranger among a people who did not understand and had no good reason to understand me and my people. . . . In other words, it was a pretty difficult business to be a Filipino in the United States in the years preceding Pearl Harbor."

But in many places it was still a "difficult business" even after Pearl Harbor. Many whites continued to treat Filipinos as strangers. Stationed at Camp Beale in California, soldiers of the First Filipino Infantry Regiment found they were unwelcome in the nearby town of Marysville. Dressed proudly in their army uniforms, several Filipino soldiers went into town one weekend, planning to have a good dinner and see the sights. They went into a restaurant and sat down, but no one came to serve them. After waiting for half an hour, one of them got up and asked for service. He was told, "We don't serve Filipinos here." Filipino soldiers were turned away from theaters or were forced to sit in a segregated section, away from the white patrons. Wives who visited them could not get rooms at the hotels.

When the colonel who commanded the regiment heard about the discrimination against his men, he met with the Marysville Chamber of Commerce. "There," said Manuel Buaken, a private in the regiment, "he laid down the law of cooperation with the army—or else. Then the merchants and the restaurant proprietors and the movie houses changed their tune," and opened their businesses to the Filipinos. But the "soul of enjoyment" was gone for Buaken and his fellow soldiers. They knew that in their hearts the merchants and waiters were hating and ridiculing the Filipinos, laughing at their brown skin. And the Filipino soldiers hoped they would soon be gone from "these towns which hate built" and "this land of double-talk."

Slowly, however, the war began to open the way for Filipinos. Above all, it let many of them claim citizenship. As members of the U.S. armed forces, they were allowed to become American citizens. On February 20, 1943, on the parade ground of Camp Beale, 1,200 Filipino soldiers stood proudly and silently in formation during the ceremony of citizenship. Their colonel said, "Officers who returned from Bataan have said there are no finer soldiers in the world than the Filipinos who fought and starved and died there shoulder to shoulder with our troops. I can well believe it as I look at the men before me. On those faces is quiet determination and a consciousness of training and discipline with a definite end in view. I congratulate them on their soldierly appearance and on their approaching citizenship." In the concluding speech, a judge welcomed the Filipinos, saying, "Citizenship came to us who were born here as a heritage—it will come to you as a privilege. We have every faith you will become and remain loyal, devoted citizens of the United States."

Filipino guerrillas prepare to join a victory parade after the liberation of Luzon Island from Japanese occupation.

Before the war, laws in California and other states had prevented Asian immigrants from owning land. In the early 1940s, however, the attorney general of California studied the state's land laws and decided that Filipinos could be allowed to lease land. He encouraged them to take over the land that had belonged to U.S. residents of Japanese descent, who had been sent to internment centers during the war because it was thought that they might pose a threat to military security on

the West Coast. Fearful of being mistaken for Japanese, who
were hated and feared, Filipinos took pains to identify themselves. A Filipino woman recalled her mother's instructions
soon after the beginning of the war: "My mother told me to
make sure you say you're not Japanese if they ask you who
you are. Filipinos wore buttons saying, 'I am a Filipino.'"

Manuel Buaken welcomed the internment of the Japanese Americans and the changes in the laws that let Filipinos
become citizens and lease land. Buaken felt that the Japanese
immigrants, by teaching their children Japanese and creating
their own business communities, had shown that they were
not really interested in becoming part of American society.
Filipinos, however, were ready and eager to blend in, as
Buaken explained: "We have always wanted nothing more
than to learn from America, to become good Americans. We
have developed no great banks here in the United States—our
savings have gone into American banks. We have patronized
American stores—not stores devoted to the selling of prod-
ucts from across the seas. We have striven to learn English,
not to perpetuate foreign language schools and to teach
foreign ideas to our children." Sadly, Buaken's ideas grew out
of anti-Japanese feelings, not out of America's democratic
ideals.

These democratic ideals had to be more sharply defined during the war. Because the United States was fighting
dictatorship in other countries, America's leaders felt that
America must make good its claims to democracy. Some steps
were taken toward equal rights. In 1941, President Roosevelt
issued an executive order that outlawed racial discrimination
in the workplace. The order said, "It is the duty of employers
and labor organizations . . . to provide for full and equitable

participation of all workers in defense industries, without discrimination because of race, creed, color, or national origin." At the same time, new job opportunities opened up for Filipinos because the war industries needed workers. Filipinos found jobs in shipyards and munitions factories. Shortly before he left to fight in the Pacific, one Filipino remarked, "In the United States, the war is doing wonders for the resident Filipinos."

Soon after the war ended in 1945, the U.S. Congress passed a law that allowed Filipino immigrants to become citizens. "It took a war and a great calamity in our country to bring us [whites and Filipinos] together," observed Carlos Bulosan. The new law also increased the number of Filipino immigrants who could enter the United States each year from

The war opened the door to citizenship for some immigrants. Twelve hundred members of the First Filipino Infantry Regiment became U.S. citizens in a mass ceremony at Camp Beale, California.

50 to 100, which became the annual quota after the Philippines received full independence in 1946.

Meanwhile, a social scientist studied how the war had changed the status of Filipinos. He noted that as the Japanese left Los Angeles, Filipinos bought homes from them in the more desirable neighborhoods. Many Filipinos also bought small farms from the Japanese in California's agricultural districts. Job opportunities expanded for Filipinos. They entered shipyards and manufacturing plants as welders, technicians, assembly or office workers, and, in a few cases, engineers. The war had also forced Filipinos to make a decision—"to go home and help in the reconstruction of their homeland" or "to spend the rest of their days in America." Thousands of Filipinos, granted citizenship and feeling a sense of greater acceptance, chose to make America their permanent home. But would whites forget Bataan when the war faded from memory and economic growth slowed down, bringing hard times again? Would Filipino Americans be doomed to another "interminable era of dish washing and asparagus cutting"?

Filipinos had reason to be doubtful. They had finally been granted citizenship, but they knew that their new status did not mean that white Americans truly accepted them. "What good would it do to become citizens of America," asked a Filipino soldier, "if we are still brown-skin inferiors?" Filipinos could not change their complexion. To some white people, they would remain just "Orientals." The struggle for equality and acceptance was not yet over.

Lieutenant Young O. Kim, a Korean American member of the 34th
Infantry Division, is decorated for gallantry in the Italian campaign
by General Mark W. Clark.

Chapter Three

"*I Am Korean*"

ON THE MORNING OF DECEMBER 7, SOME KOREANS IN LOS Angeles were rehearsing for a play. They were putting on the show to raise money to help 200,000 refugee Korean families living in China and also to support Korean volunteers who were fighting the Japanese. Their rehearsal was suddenly interrupted by an electrifying announcement: "The Japanese have attacked Pearl Harbor." At once, everyone on the stage cried, *"Taehan toknip manse!"* ("Long live Korean independence!")

One of the players, Bong-Youn Choy, later recalled, "No Korean, old and young alike, could control his emotions of joy. Every Korean felt that the long dream for national independence would soon become a reality." The bombing of Pearl Harbor meant that the United States would enter the war against Japan. Koreans in the United States, especially first-generation immigrants with strong ties to their homeland, hoped that the United States would drive the Japanese out of Korea, which they had held for nearly 40 years. War would bring destruction and death, they knew, but perhaps it would also bring freedom.

That night, Koreans gathered at the Korean National Association in Los Angeles to discuss how they would act during the war. They agreed to make every effort to contribute to the American war effort. Some would volunteer for the National Guard; others would buy war bonds; still others would offer their skills—for example, Koreans who spoke Japanese could help the U.S. armed forces by serving as translators and interpreters.

Although Korean patriots welcomed the war, hoping that the United States and its allies would crush Japan and bring about Korean independence, for many Koreans in America the war years were a time of painful confusion. They watched with mixed feelings as their Japanese American neighbors, many of whom had been born in the United States, were treated as spies and enemy agents. Among white Americans, anti-Japanese feeling reached its peak in February 1942, when President Roosevelt signed an order that allowed Japanese Americans in California, Oregon, and Washington to be interned, or placed in guarded camps during the war.

A Korean American woman named Jean Park recalled the upheaval that World War II brought into Asian American lives. She and her family were living in California when the war broke out. A few months after the attack on Pearl Harbor, she began to hear stories that the Japanese were being taken to the camps. "People said that the Japanese were treated very cruelly and that they were dragged to unknown destinations," she recalled. When the Japanese were taken to the camps, opportunities opened up for Koreans. For example, Jean Park's stepfather moved the family to southern California where "the Japanese lost all their farms and many of the farms were being sold for very cheap prices."

But when Jean and her family arrived at their new home, they found whites staring at them and shouting, "Japs go home!" Like many other Korean Americans, the Parks had been mistaken for Japanese. Said Jean of the townspeople, "They were ready to stone us with rocks and descend on us because they had that evil look in their eyes." To protect themselves from anti-Japanese violence, Koreans wore badges showing the Korean flag or the statement "I am a Korean." They put similar stickers on their cars.

Even the U.S. government sometimes failed to distinguish Koreans from Japanese. Because Japan controlled Korea,

U.S. law said that Korean immigrants were subjects of Japan. This meant that in 1941, after the United States declared war against Japan, the American government identified Koreans in the United States as "enemy aliens." In February 1942, the *Korean National Herald–Pacific Weekly* insisted that the government identify Koreans as Koreans. "The Korean is an enemy of Japan," the paper declared. "Since December 7, the Korean here is between the devil and the deep sea for the reason that the United States considers him a subject of Japan, which the Korean resents as an injustice to his true status. . . . What is the status of a Korean in the United States? Is he an enemy alien? Has any Korean ever been in Japanese espionage or in subversive activities against the land where he makes his home and rears his children as true Americans?"

In May 1942, Korean Americans marched in Los Angeles for victory and the independence of Korea.

In Hawaii, Koreans were also classified as enemy aliens. Korean immigrants who worked on defense projects in the islands had to wear black-bordered badges that identified them as Japanese subjects. "For years we've been fighting the Japanese and now they tell us that we're Japs. It's an insult!" Koreans snapped angrily. "Why in the hell do they pull a trick like this on us," the Korean workers screamed, "when we hate the Japanese more than anyone else in the world?" After their protests, they still had to wear the badges, but they were allowed to add the words "I am Korean."

Not all Koreans viewed the Japanese Americans as the enemy. Many young Koreans sympathized with the Japanese Americans on the West Coast who lost their homes and jobs when they were interned in the camps. "It made me feel sad to hear that their land was taken away from them," said Jean Park, "and that they were imprisoned." In Hawaii, second-

Koreans in the United States made heroic contributions to the war effort. These Korean men formed a California unit of the National Guard. Their officers, however, were white.

generation Koreans did not think of the local Japanese people as their enemies. A young Korean man explained that the bombing of Pearl Harbor did not change his feelings toward his Japanese neighbors and acquaintances. "We've lived with them all along and know them well and it didn't occur to me that they were responsible," he said.

Some Koreans viewed the matter in a more sinister light. Months before Pearl Harbor, a leader in the Korean independence movement declared that 35,000 to 50,000 Japanese in Hawaii were ready to help Japan in a war against the United States. The same Korean spokesman also claimed that the Japanese Americans on the West Coast were spying for Japan. These charges were not true, but they reflected the mistrust and hostility that many Koreans, especially the older immigrants, felt toward all Japanese.

Korean immigrants were eager to contribute to the American war effort against Japan. Many of them had an invaluable weapon which the country needed: they knew the Japanese language. During the war, they taught Japanese to American soldiers and translated captured Japanese documents. They also made radio broadcasts in Japanese to undermine support for Japan in the Pacific nations, and they served as secret agents in parts of Asia that were occupied by Japanese forces.

In Los Angeles, 109 Koreans—one-fifth of the city's Korean population—joined the National Guard. Ranging in age from 18 to 65, they were organized into a Korean unit called the Tiger Brigade. They drilled regularly on Saturday and Sunday afternoons in Exposition Park, preparing to defend California against an enemy invasion. A white army officer congratulated the men of the Tiger Brigade, saying, "I

The people of a Korean village greet arriving American soldiers. Japan's defeat in the war brought independence to Korea, but at the cost of dividing the country into two parts.

myself have learned the real meaning of patriotism during my participation in this Tiger Brigade, and I cannot find adequate words to describe your contribution in winning this war." Elderly Koreans, too, made their contributions, the women serving in the Red Cross and the men volunteering as emergency fire wardens. Koreans in Hawaii and on the mainland bought defense bonds to help pay for the war effort. In 1942–43, they bought more than $239,000 worth of bonds—an immense sum for a population of only 10,000 people.

Their involvement in the war effort earned the Koreans new respect from white Americans. At the celebration of Korean National Flag Day on August 29, 1943, the mayor of Los Angeles raised the Korean flag to honor the uniformed men of the Tiger Brigade as they marched past City Hall. A year later, a congressman from Hawaii tried to get Congress to pass a law that would let Korean immigrants become U.S. citizens. He failed, however; the United States was not yet ready to grant citizenship to Asians. But the fact that he had tried was proof that Koreans were gaining greater acceptance in American society.

As the Koreans in America had hoped, World War II did bring about the end of Japanese rule in Korea, although not in the way that the Korean patriots had expected. Korea was liberated by United States forces who entered from the south and Soviet forces who entered from the north. Each of these superpowers had its own ideas about the kind of government that should be established in Korea, so the country was divided into two parts in 1948. North Korea, or the Democratic People's Republic of Korea, became a communist state supported by its powerful communist neighbors, the Soviet Union and the People's Republic of China. South Korea, called the Republic of Korea, was backed by the United States. This division of Korea into two zones administered by foreign powers was a sad blow to Korean Americans who had hoped that their homeland would become fully independent as soon as the war ended.

A World War II recruiting poster in India. American and British leaders feared that India might be vulnerable to a Japanese invasion.

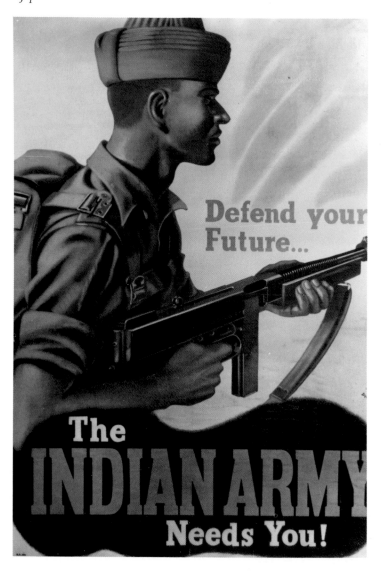

Chapter Four

Opening the Door of Democracy

ON THE EVE OF AMERICA'S ENTRY INTO WORLD WAR II, Asian Indians in the United States were struggling for the right to become citizens. Like other immigrant groups from Asia, they had suffered setbacks at the hands of the exclusionists—white Americans who wanted to exclude, or keep out, immigrants who were not white Europeans.

Asian Indians had come to America in far smaller numbers than Chinese, Japanese, Korean, or Filipino immigrants. Only about 6,400 of them had entered the United States by 1920. Most came from the Punjab, a region of northwestern India. In America they were called Hindus, but actually some were followers of Islam, and most belonged to the Sikh faith—a blending of Hinduism and Islam.

The Asian Indians posed a special problem for America's exclusionists. Many scholars agreed that the people of India belonged to the Caucasian race, the same large category of human types that included whites but did *not* include the Chinese, Japanese, and other Asian peoples. Yet while some Asian Indians were light skinned, and many had features similar to those of Europeans, others were dark skinned and seemed closer in appearance to Africans or East Asians. In addition, the cultures of India were as alien to most white Americans as the cultures of China and Japan. But unlike the Chinese and Japanese, who looked different from whites *and* belonged to a different race, Asian Indians were viewed as members of the Caucasian race. This raised the question of whether Asian Indians could become citizens of the United States.

A federal law dating from 1790 said that only "white persons" could become naturalized citizens. (The process by which immigrants become citizens of their new country is

47

called naturalization, and immigrants who receive citizenship are called naturalized citizens.) This 1790 law had prevented Chinese, Japanese, Korean, and Filipino immigrants from claiming U.S. citizenship. But Asian Indians said that the law did not apply to them. They believed that the words "white persons" meant "persons belonging to the Caucasian race." Asian Indians were Caucasians and therefore should be allowed to become naturalized citizens.

This tangled question of race and citizenship went all the way to the U.S. Supreme Court in 1923. An immigrant from India named Bhagat Singh Thind argued that as a member of the Caucasian race, he was eligible for citizenship. The Court destroyed the hopes of Thind and his fellow immigrants, however, by ruling that the term "white person" meant an immigrant from northern or western Europe. Although Asian Indians and Europeans might have come from a common stock "in the dim reaches of antiquity," said the Court, they were now separate. In the view of the "common man," Asian Indians were not "white persons." Their bid for citizenship was turned down. In addition, they were turned away from government aid programs during the severe economic depression of the 1930s because they were aliens who were not eligible for citizenship.

Their hopes dashed by the *Thind* case and the Great Depression, some Asian Indian immigrants returned to India. By 1940, according to the U.S. census, the Asian Indian population in the United States numbered only 2,400. Their numbers had dwindled, but they had not abandoned their quest for equal rights. The outbreak of World War II—called by the United States "the war to defend democracy"—

strengthened the Asian Indians' demand for equality in America.

Under the leadership of Mubarak Ali Khan, the India Welfare League protested against discrimination and asked Congress for help. In 1939, even before the United States joined the war, a bill was introduced in Congress to give citizenship to all Asian Indian immigrants who had lived in the United States since 1924. The bill was attacked by the American Federation of Labor (AFL), which wanted to keep foreign laborers out of the country. A spokesman for the AFL

Like other Asian immigrants, people from India were victims of racial discrimination in the United States. The war sharpened Americans' awareness of the problem. Fighting oppression abroad, could they continue to tolerate prejudice at home?

warned Congress, "First, it will be the people who are here in our country now, the Chinese, Japanese, and Hindus, who want to be naturalized. Then they will find some other means of breaking some other little hole in the immigration law here and there or elsewhere."

Unwilling to wait for Congress to act, Khairata Ram Samras turned to the law. In 1940, he filed a petition in the federal court of San Francisco challenging the *Thind* decision. He argued that it was a violation of the Constitution for the United States to deny citizenship to Asian Indian immigrants. But the congressional bill failed to pass, and Samras's challenge was rejected by the court.

A year later, in August 1941, President Roosevelt and Winston Churchill, the prime minister of Great Britain, issued a document called the Atlantic Charter. It was a statement of democratic principles, including the right of peoples to choose their own form of government. Asian Indians realized that the Atlantic Charter gave them an opportunity to press for their rights in the United States. Mubarak Ali Khan of the India Welfare League and Sirdar Jagit Singh of the India League of America demanded two things: independence for India, which was then a colony of Great Britain, and naturalization rights for Asian Indians in the United States.

The war gave a boost to the Asian Indians' demand for fairer treatment. America's leaders saw that the United States needed India's help in the war against Japan. India was located in a position of great strategic importance, midway between Japan and Europe. The Allies feared that Japan might push its campaign westward and try to join forces with Germany somewhere in western Asia. Many people in India were opposed to British rule in their country, and the Allies were afraid that Japan would play upon this opposition, create political chaos in Calcutta and other Indian cities, and drive its military machinery across India. The United States and the other Allied nations realized that they depended upon India to block any such Japanese advance. To win favor among the people of India, the U.S. Congress decided to listen to the complaints of Asian Indians in America. In March of 1944, Congress introduced a bill that would allow immigrants from India to enter the United States and become citizens. The bill was supported by a congressman from New York, who claimed that oppressed people throughout the world looked to the United States for justice and equality. But Japanese propaganda was painting a picture of the United States as a place of prejudice and unfairness. By "breaking down" the barriers against immigration and naturalization, the congressman argued, America could prove Japan wrong.

Four months later, an Asian Indian scholar named S. Chandrasekhar, a lecturer at the University of Pennsylvania, outlined another reason for Congress to pass the bill. He wrote that the United States must fight Nazi ideas about racial superiority. Pointing out that Germany claimed the right to oppress the other peoples of Europe because they were "inferior," Chandrasekhar added:

> If the United States is successfully to combat such dangerous ideas, it can ill afford to practice racial discrimination in its relations with Asiatic countries. The immigration policy of this country now excludes nearly a quarter of the human race. America cannot

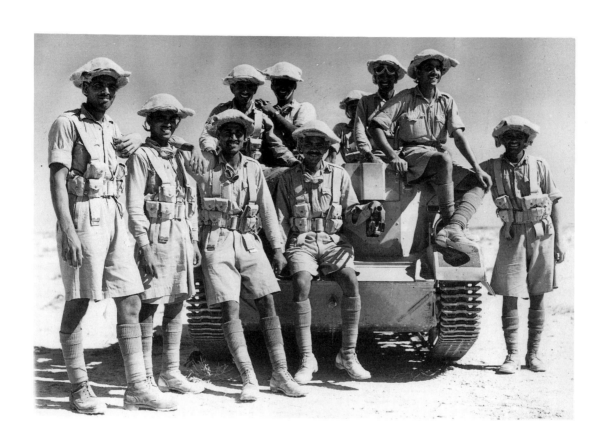

Indian troops served with the British army in Asia and North Africa.

afford to say that she wants the people of India to fight on her side and at the same time maintain that she will not have them among her immigrant groups.

The United States could not have it both ways. It could not oppose the racism of the Nazis abroad and also practice racism at home. America had to live up to its "principle of equality," Chandrasekhar said, to keep faith with the millions of people in India who looked to America for "justice and fair play."

Two years later, in 1946, Congress acted. It permitted a few new immigrants from India to enter the United States each year, and it also let Asian Indians become naturalized citizens. In the 18 years that followed, 12,000 Indians entered the United States. One historian of immigration wrote that if Congress had not changed the law in 1946, the Asian Indian community in the United States might have become extinct.

Nearly 1,800 Asian Indians became U.S. citizens between 1947 and 1965. One of them was Dalip Singh Saund, who had come to America from the Punjab in 1919. Saund had become a successful farmer in California's Imperial Valley. For decades he had wanted to become a citizen. "I had married an American girl, and was the father of three American children," he explained in his autobiography. "I was making America my home. Thus it was only natural that I felt very uncomfortable not being able to become a citizen of the United States." Citizenship was more than a matter of political rights for Saund. It also let him own his land. "I saw that the bars of citizenship were shut tight against me," Saund said. "I knew if these bars were lifted I would see much wider gates of opportunity open to me, opportunity as existed for everybody else in the United States of America." After Saund became a naturalized citizen, he went on to be elected to the House of Representatives in 1956, serving for three terms. The war had opened the door of democracy to Saund and other Asian Indian Americans.

A resident of New York's Chinatown wears a pin displaying the American and Chinese flags. After Japan bombed Pearl Harbor, many Chinese Americans wore such buttons so that they would not be mistaken for Japanese.

"I REMEMBER DECEMBER 7TH SO CLEARLY," SAID LONNIE Quan of San Francisco four decades later. "I was living at Gum Moon Residence Club on Washington Street. It was Sunday. I didn't have a radio in the room." Quan's boyfriend came over, excitedly exclaiming, "This is it. Pearl Harbor was attacked!" The news was overwhelming. "I just couldn't believe it—it was a shock," said Quan. "I remember going to work in a restaurant, Cathay House, and everybody was just kinda glued to the radio."

The next day, the United States declared war on Japan and became an ally of China. Two weeks later, in an article filled with false racial stereotypes, *Time* magazine told their white readers how to tell their Chinese "friends" from the Japanese "enemy":

> HOW TO TELL YOUR FRIENDS FROM THE JAPS: Virtually all Japanese are short. Japanese are likely to be stockier and broader-hipped than short Chinese. Japanese are seldom fat; they often dry up and grow lean as they age. Although both have the typical epicanthic fold of the upper eyelid, Japanese eyes are usually set closer together. The Chinese expression is likely to be more placid, kindly, open; the Japanese more positive, dogmatic, arrogant. Japanese are hesitant, nervous in conversation, laugh loudly at the wrong time. Japanese walk stiffly erect, hard heeled. Chinese, more relaxed, have an easy gait, sometimes shuffle.

This article represented a sudden change in the way Chinese were viewed in the United States. For years Chinese had been feared and insulted. Now they were friends and allies engaged in a heroic shared battle against the Japanese.

For a long time the Chinese had been regarded with scorn. "Then came Pearl Harbor, December 7," said a congressman in 1943. "All at once we discovered the saintly qualities of the Chinese people. If it had not been for December 7, I do not know if we would have ever found out how good they were." But the *Time* article and the chorus of praise gave the Chinese little confidence that they would not still be mistaken for the enemy. They remembered how many times they had been called "Japs." They knew that whites simply lumped all Asians together. Fearful of anti-Japanese hate and violence, many Chinese shopkeepers displayed signs announcing, "This is a Chinese shop." In the Chinese community, thousands of buttons were distributed. They read, "I am Chinese."

> *When World War II was declared*
> *on the morning radio,*
> *we glued our ears, widened our eyes.*
> *Our bodies shivered. . . .*
> *Shortly our Japanese neighbors vanished*
> *and my parents continued to whisper:*
> *We are Chinese, we are Chinese.*
> *We wore black arm bands,*
> *put up a sign*
> *in bold letters.*

The outbreak of the war sharpened the attachment of Chinese immigrants to their homeland. They worried about loved ones they had left behind, and they waited anxiously for

news from China, carried in letters such as this one from a nephew to his uncle in America:

> Uncle, Venerable One, I write to you with respectful greeting:
>
> I received ten dollars from Hong Kong money from you lately. I thank you very much. How I would like to see you come home and be with us in the near future, too.
>
> Now Canton is captured by the Japs, our commodities here cannot be shipped to the village. For this reason, the prices of foodstuff in the village are high, very high. One bag of rice costs from eight to nine dollars. How can the poor families back home manage to live! However, everybody at home is well. I hope you are well, too, in America.

In a short story called "One Mother's Day," published in May 1941 in the *China Daily News* of New York City, Lao

The Chinese Benevolent Association passes out identification buttons in New York. Chinese Americans were treated with new respect during the war, but they wondered if white America's friendliness would outlast the war.

57

Mei described the feelings of a restaurant worker in Chinatown. Living as a "wanderer" in America, he is seized one day
by thoughts of home. He thinks of his "invaded home village,"
especially his 70-year-old mother. As he walks the streets of
New York, he worries about what has become of her. "How
about a fresh flower for your mother on Mother's Day?" asks
an old woman with a basket full of flowers. The man is
startled, "as if someone had discovered his inner secrets." He
buys a red flower and a white one, pins them to his lapel, and
walks toward the park.

Like this homesick restaurant worker, Chinese in
America were reminded by the war of their deep family ties
to their homeland. They also felt a new patriotic closeness to
the United States, their adopted home. When America entered the war, celebrations broke out in Chinatowns across
the country. The San Francisco Chinese community published
a message to Germany and Japan:

> Have you heard the bad news? America is out to get
> you. America has a grim, but enthusiastic bombing
> party started, and you're the target in the parlor game.
> San Francisco Chinatown, U.S.A., is joining the party.
> Chinatown will have fun blasting you to hell. China-
> town is proud to be a part of Freedom's legion in
> freeing all the decent people of the world from your
> spectacle.
> Chinatown's part of the party will cost $500,000.
> Admission price to the fun is purchase of a U.S. War
> Bond. We're all going to buy a War Bond for Victory.
> P. S. More bad news. Everyone in Chinatown is going
> to this party. We're NOT missing this one.

In San Francisco, the Chinese contributed generously to the defense of America, raising money for the Red Cross and for the Defense Bond Drive, which helped pay for the war effort. In New York's Chinatown, excited crowds cheered themselves hoarse when the first Chinese Americans were drafted into the U.S. Army. Chinese American boys, too young for the armed services, tried to join by giving their "Chinese age," which was usually a year or two older than the age shown on their birth certificates.

Everyone in the Chinese community, including women and children, took part in the war effort. In an essay published in the *Chinese Press* in 1942, teenager Florence Gee proudly described her family's involvement: "I am an American. . . . The war has hit home. I have an uncle in the army and one in the shipyard. My sisters are members of the civilian defense. My mother is taking first aid. I belong to a club where I learn better citizenship." In Minneapolis, the owner of the city's only Chinese gift shop closed his business during the busiest part of the Christmas season to join his wife as a worker in a war-industry plant. Actress Anna May Wong signed up as an air-raid warden in Santa Monica, California. "As an American-born Chinese," she said, "I feel it is a privilege to be able to do my little bit in return for the many advantages bestowed upon me by a free democracy."

Young Chinese Americans were eager to wear American military uniforms. "To men of my generation," explained Charlie Leong of San Francisco's Chinatown, "World War II was the most important historic event of our times. For the first time we felt we could make it in American society." The war gave them the chance to get out of Chinatown, put on army uniforms, and be sent overseas, where they felt "they were part of the great patriotic United States war machine out to do battle with the enemy." Harold Liu of New York's Chinatown later recalled, "In the 1940s for the first time Chinese were accepted by Americans as being friends because at that time, Chinese and Americans were fighting against the Japanese and the Germans and the Nazis. Therefore, all of a sudden, we became part of an American dream. . . . It was just a whole different era and in the community we began to feel very good about ourselves. . . . My own brother went into the service. We were so proud that they were in uniform." Altogether, 13,500 Chinese entered the U.S. armed forces—22% of all Chinese men in America.

Even those who did not fight were affected by the war. For years their job opportunities had been limited. Most of

Shipyard workers in New Jersey brandish their welding rods in a "V for Victory" sign. The labor needs of the defense industries gave many Chinese Americans their first chance to work outside Chinatown.

*A worker on the Pacific
Coast leaves onlookers
without doubt about his
ethnic identity.*

them could find work only in Chinese-owned laundries and restaurants. After the war started, better jobs opened to them. They were especially welcome in defense industries such as aircraft and munitions factories, where there was a shortage of labor. Waiters left the restaurants and rushed to the higher-paying industrial jobs. Some Chinese restaurants had to shut down because of a lack of waiters, and in Los Angeles 300 Chinese laundry workers closed their shops to help build the ship *China Victory*. Fifteen percent of all shipyard workers in the San Francisco Bay Area in 1943 were Chinese. Chinese also found jobs in the shipyards of Washington State, Delaware, Mississippi, and in airplane factories on Long Island.

One of these new defense industry workers was Arthur Wong. After arriving in New York's Chinatown in 1930 at the age of 17, he found he could not get a job outside the Chinese community. "I worked five and a half days in the laundry and worked the whole weekend in the restaurant," he said. "And then came the war, and defense work opened up; and some of my friends went to work in a defense plant, and they recommended that I should apply for defense work. So I went to work for Curtiss-Wright, making airplanes. I started out as an assembler, as a riveter." Thousands of laundrymen and waiters like Wong were finally given the chance to break away from Chinatown. The *Chinese Press* estimated that nearly a third of the Chinese American young men in New York City were working in defense plants. In addition, many college-educated Chinese were now able to find work in their fields of training, such as architecture and engineering.

The war also opened opportunities for Chinese American women like Jade Snow Wong. After graduating from college, Wong had trouble finding a good job. She was discriminated against on two counts: because she was Chinese and because she was a woman. Then the war industries began to demand workers. "By this time the trek to the shipyards was well underway," wrote Wong. "The patriotic fever to build as many ships as possible, together with boom wages, combined to attract people from all types of occupations." Wong was hired as a typist-clerk in a shipyard in Marin County, California. Several hundred "alert young Chinese American girls," the *Chinese Press* reported in 1942, "have gone to the defense industries as office workers." The paper

proudly listed some of these women workers and added, "They're part of the millions who stand behind the man behind the gun." A year later, in an article on "Women in the War," the *Chinese Press* told its readers about Alice Yick, Boston Navy Yard's only Chinese woman mechanical trainee, who could run light lathes, grinders, and other machine tools. "Helen Young, Lucy Young, and Hilda Lee," the paper continued, "were the first Chinese women aircraft workers in California. They help build B-24 bombers in San Diego."

In 1942, a social scientist named Rose Hum Lee happily recorded the ways the war was changing the lives of

Residents of San Francisco's Chinatown gather in front of the Chinese Times *newspaper office to read bulletins about the war in China.*

Chinese in the United States. "They have gone in the army and navy, into shipbuilding and aircraft plants," Lee wrote. "Even the girls are getting jobs." But while Chinese were joining in the American war effort, Lee noted, they were not fully equal. Laws prevented new Chinese immigrants from entering the United States, and those already in the country were not allowed to become citizens. Lee argued that Chinese should be treated just like European immigrants. Like newcomers from Europe, they should be able to become naturalized citizens. Lee then pointed out that it was not fair for America to subject its own allies and partners to racism. She wrote: "Surely racial discrimination should not be directed against those who are America's Allies in the Far East and are helping her in every way to win the war. . . . To be fighting for freedom and democracy in the Far East, at the cost of seven million lives in five years of hard, long, bitter warfare, and to be denied equal opportunity in the greatest of democracies, seems the height of irony." The contrast between America's claim to be a democracy and its racist treatment of the Chinese was embarrassing. It should not be allowed to continue.

The war abroad required reform at home, many Americans began to realize. In 1942, the California League of Women Voters of San Francisco started a campaign to remove racial discrimination from the immigration laws. A year later, Congress began considering a bill that would repeal, or cancel, the law that excluded Chinese immigrants. But this plan fanned the fire of anti-Chinese fear and hostility. The American Federation of Labor warned that the bill would open the gates for an invasion of laborers from Asia who would take jobs away from white Americans.

Despite such fears, the pressure mounted on the government to repeal the law against Chinese immigration. Spokespeople for the Chinese government toured the United States, explaining that the repeal of the exclusion law would boost the war effort in China. Chinese Americans, too, worked hard to get the bill passed. Theodora Chan Wang of the Chinese Women's Association of New York wrote a letter to Eleanor Roosevelt, wife of the president, urging the passage of the bill. The Chinese Consolidated Benevolent Association of New York asked Congress to repeal the exclusion law, calling the law a serious violation of the equality and friendship between the two nations. In Hawaii, Chinese Americans raised money for the campaign for repeal. And at a conference in Texas in September 1943, more than 70 Chinese young people condemned the exclusion law as "the stumbling block between China and America," and urged their American friends to repeal it at once, not to wait until the war was over.

The Korean and Asian Indian communities also wanted to see the law against Chinese immigration repealed. Representatives of these groups declared that *all* Asians sought political and economic equality with their fellow Americans. An immigrant from India who was a college professor in New York reminded Congress that America could not promote democracy abroad and remain racist at home. He explained that as long as the United States practiced racial discrimination against Asian peoples, very few Asians would believe America's claims to support world democracy and world brotherhood.

President Roosevelt felt the pressure. He sent Congress a message favoring the repeal bill. "China is our ally,"

*Brothers in arms, a Chinese
American (left) and a
Japanese American soldier
in the U.S. Army share a
moment of relaxation on
Okinawa, the scene of bitter
fighting against Japan.*

Roosevelt wrote. "For many long years she stood alone in the fight against aggression. Today we fight at her side. She has continued her gallant struggle against very great odds." The president urged Congress to "be big enough" to admit that the Chinese exclusion laws had been a mistake. "By the repeal of the Chinese exclusion laws," he wrote, "we can correct a historic mistake and silence the distorted Japanese propaganda."

Japan had been calling to Asians to unite in a race war against white America. Japanese propaganda condemned the United States for its discriminatory laws and for the way Chinese in America were limited to low-paying jobs and treated with hostility or ridicule. "Far from waging this war to liberate the oppressed peoples of the world," Japan argued on the radio waves, "the Anglo-American leaders are trying to restore the obsolete system of imperialism." The Japanese claimed that the U.S. Congress never seriously intended to pass the repeal bill. America would never reopen its doors to Chinese immigrants. According to Japan, the repeal bill was "only a gesture, empty words."

If the bill did not pass, Japan would mock and scorn the United States before a watching audience of millions in Asia, said supporters of the bill. They argued, "It is time for us to realize that if nations cannot be gracious to each other, cannot respect each other's race, all talk of democracy is in vain."

Congress listened to these arguments. In late 1943, the Chinese exclusion law was repealed. Chinese immigrants could once again enter the United States. In reality, the new law allowed only a tiny trickle of immigration from China: no more than 105 Chinese could enter each year. But the law did open the way for Chinese to become U.S. citizens. Those living in the United States could apply for naturalization if they could prove that they had entered the country legally; they also had to pass tests in their ability to use the English language and on American history and the U.S. Constitution.

One of the 1,400 Chinese immigrants who won their citizenship between 1944 and 1952 was Jade Snow Wong's father. "At the age of seventy plus, after years of attending night classes in citizenship, he became naturalized," his daughter joyfully reported. "He embraced this status whole-heartedly. One day when we were discussing plans for his birthday celebration, which was usually observed on the tenth day of the fifth lunar month by the Chinese calendar, he announced, 'Now that I have become a United States citizen, I am going to change my birthday. Henceforth, it will be on the Fourth of July.'"

In Hawaii, hundreds of citizens of Japanese ancestry volunteered for combat against Japan.

"ONE MORNING—I THINK IT WAS A SUNDAY—WHILE I was working at Palama Shoe Factory I heard, *'Pon! pon! Pon! pon!'*" recalled a Japanese resident of Hawaii. He was only a few miles away from the U.S. navy base at Pearl Harbor. "I was drinking coffee and I thought, 'Strange. Are they having military practice?' At the corner of Liliha and Kuakini streets, a bomb fell in the back of a cement plant. We felt like going to see what happened, the noise was so loud. We found out that the war had started."

The bombs that fell on Hawaii on December 7, 1941, echoed loudly throughout America. They killed more than 2,000 people and destroyed many military ships and planes. Americans were stunned and angered by this attack on their territory, and in the wake of Pearl Harbor, they felt hostility toward everything and everyone Japanese. On the mainland, more than 120,000 people of Japanese descent were interned—that is, rounded up and put into guarded camps. Many of them had been born in the United States and were therefore American citizens.

The Japanese people of Hawaii were spared the nightmare of internment. While Asians on the mainland had remained "strangers" in a mostly white society, the Japanese and other Asians in Hawaii had become "locals." About 158,000 people of Japanese descent lived in Hawaii, making up 37% of the islands' population.

Shortly after inspecting the still-smoking ruins at Pearl Harbor, Navy Secretary Frank Knox declared that the Japanese in Hawaii had helped plan and carry out the attack. He was wrong. Investigators from the military and the Federal Bureau of Investigation (FBI) all agreed that no such sabotage had occurred. But Knox's alarming announcement fueled rumors of sabotage committed by Japanese Americans in the islands. Wild rumors said that Japanese plantation laborers had cut arrows in the sugar cane and pineapple fields to guide the Japanese bombers, and that Japanese in Hawaii had given signals to enemy planes. Several weeks after the attack, Knox said that the Japanese should be rounded up and interned on one of the outer islands.

Knox's plan was blocked by General Delos Emmons, the military governor of Hawaii. Emmons said in a radio broadcast, "There is no intention or desire on the part of the federal authorities to operate mass concentration camps. No person, be he citizen or alien, need worry, provided he is not connected with subversive elements. . . . While we have been subjected to a serious attack by a ruthless and treacherous enemy, we must remember that this is America and we must do things the American Way. We must distinguish between loyalty and disloyalty among our people."

Emmons also told the U.S. War Department that it would be a mistake to intern the Japanese. The construction materials and workers that would be needed to build internment camps were more urgently needed for other wartime tasks, and soldiers could not be spared to guard the Japanese. He also pointed out that the Japanese were vitally important on the island of Oahu, where Hawaii's capital city of Honolulu is located. More than 90% of the island's carpenters, most of its transportation workers, and many of its plantation laborers were Japanese. If they were taken from their jobs, Oahu's economy would suffer. Japanese labor, Emmons said, was "absolutely essential" for rebuilding the military base at Pearl Harbor.

Emmons argued that the "Japanese question" should be handled "by those in direct contact with the situation." He believed he was in a better position to assess the threat from the local Japanese than the War Department officials, who were far away in Washington, D.C.

General Emmons remained at odds with the War Department, which continued to urge that all Japanese in Hawaii should be interned or relocated. In the end, Emmons had his way. He had seen no military reason for mass evacuation. Under his orders, only 1,444 Japanese were interned as potential threats to military security. Emmons was able to resist the federal government's pressure for mass internment partly because the people of Hawaii refused to treat the Japanese among them as enemies.

A few businessmen did favor mass relocation—not just for military security, but because they were afraid the Japanese were becoming too powerful in Hawaii. "At least 100,000 Japanese should be moved to inland mainland farming states," a telephone company official wrote to a navy admiral in August 1942. "If such a step as this was taken . . . not only the danger of internal trouble could be avoided, but the future of Hawaii would be secured against the sure political and economic domination by the Japanese within the next decade."

But most of Hawaii's *kamaaina haoles* (whites who had been in the islands a long time) were against mass internment. The president of the Honolulu Chamber of Commerce called for fair treatment of the Japanese in Hawaii, saying, "There are 160,000 of these people who want to live here because they like the country and like the American way of life. . . .

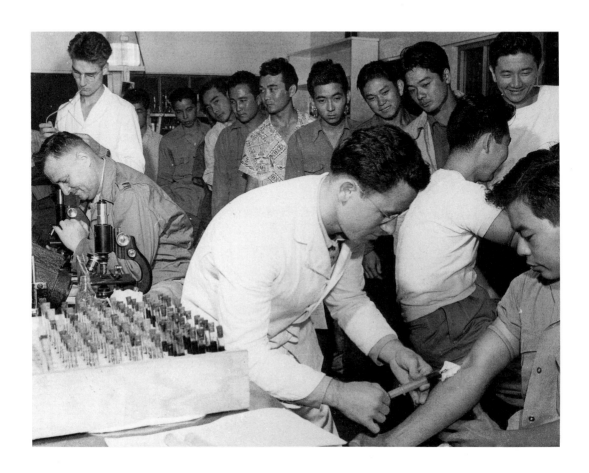

Japanese Americans undergo medical exams for entry into the armed forces. Despite wild rumors of support for Japan, military authorities in Hawaii were satisfied about the loyalty of local Japanese Americans.

The citizens of Japanese blood would fight as loyally for America as any other citizen. I have read or heard nothing in statements given out by the military, local police or FBI since December 7 to change my opinion. And I have gone out of my way to ask for the facts." The white plantation owners had a long history of living together with the Japanese in the islands and were unwilling to permit their mass uprooting. Moreover, planters knew that the removal of more than one-third of Hawaii's population would destroy the economy of the islands.

Like the business community, politicians and public officials urged restraint and reason. Hawaii's delegate to the U.S. Congress said that nothing should be done beyond arresting known spies. The Honolulu police captain denied rumors of Japanese snipers firing on American soldiers during the attack on Pearl Harbor. So did the head of the FBI in Hawaii, who said, "I want to emphasize that there was no such activity in Hawaii before, during or after the attack on Pearl Harbor. . . . I was in a position to know this fact. . . . Nowhere under the sun could there have been a more intelligent response to the needs of the hour than was given by the entire population of these islands."

When Hawaii's schools were reopened in January 1942, the school superintendent sent a message to all teachers:

> Let us be perfectly frank in recognizing the fact that the most helpless victims, emotionally and psychologically, of the present situation in Hawaii will be children of Japanese ancestry and their parents. The position of loyal American citizens of Japanese ancestry and of aliens who are unable to become naturalized, but who are nonetheless loyal to the land of their adoption, is certainly not enviable. Teachers must do everything to help the morale of these people. Let us keep constantly in mind that America is not making war on citizens of the United States or on law-abiding aliens within America.

The press in Hawaii also behaved responsibly. Newspaper editors showed confidence in the loyalty of the local Japanese, and they criticized the internment of the Japanese on the mainland. "It was an invasion of the rights of the

General Delos Emmons, military governor of Hawaii, refused to allow people of Japanese ancestry to be interned.

Japanese citizens on the Pacific coast to be picked up and shipped to the interior," wrote one editor. Newspapers also cautioned their readers not to listen to rumors, or spread them. Within days after the attack on Pearl Harbor, a Honolulu paper dismissed rumors of Japanese sabotage in the islands as "weird, amazing, and damaging untruths." A magazine called *Paradise of the Pacific* warned readers, "Beware of rumors always, avoid them like a plague and, when possible, kill them as you would a reptile. Don't repeat for a fact anything you do not know is a fact."

There were many reasons why Hawaii refused to intern its Japanese. Dollars and cents provided a strong reason—the business community did not want its labor force disrupted. Beyond that, however, the people of Hawaii had developed a multicultural society that included Americans of Japanese ancestry. In the islands, all peoples and races could become Americans.

The Japanese residents of Hawaii showed that they considered themselves to be Japanese *Americans.* During the morning of the attack, 2,000 second-generation Japanese who were serving in the U.S. Army in Hawaii fought to defend Pearl Harbor against enemy planes. Everywhere Japanese American civilians helped defend the islands. They rushed to their posts as volunteer truck drivers for the Citizens' Defense Committee. They stood in long lines in front of the hospital, waiting to give their blood to the wounded. Many of these civilians were *Issei,* first-generation immigrants. Yet, as one of them said, "Most of us have lived longer in Hawaii than in Japan. We have an obligation to this country. We are *yoshi* [adopted sons] of America. We want to do our part for America."

That night, as the people of the islands tensely waited in the darkness for the invasion they feared, thousands of Japanese American members of the Hawaii Territorial Guard—young people from the high schools and the University of Hawaii—guarded the power plants, reservoirs, and important waterfronts. For them, there was simply no doubt how they viewed the event: Japan had attacked their country. One *Nisei*, or second-generation Japanese American, had said in 1937, "As much as we would hate to see a war between the United States and Japan, and as much as we would hate to see the day come when we would have to participate in such a conflict, it would be much easier, for us I think, if such an

In Hawaii, fewer than 1,500 people of Japanese descent were fingerprinted and interned as threats to security. The vast majority of Japanese on the islands were recognized as patriotic Americans.

*The territorial guard stands
duty outside Honolulu's radio
station KGMB, fortified against
a possible Japanese invasion.*

emergency should come, to face the enemy than to stand some
of the suspicion and criticism, unjust in most cases, leveled
against us." Rather than be suspected of disloyalty, this young
man declared, he would "pack a gun and face the enemy." Four
years later, that day did come—and thousands of Nisei stood
tall in defense of their country.

"Japan's dastardly attack leaves us grim and resolute,"
declared Shunzo Sakamaki of the Oahu Citizens' Committee
for Home Defense four days after Pearl Harbor. "There is no
turning back now, no compromise with the enemy. Japan has

chosen to fight us and we'll fight." The Japanese of Hawaii
fought wholeheartedly. In June 1942, more than 1,700 Japanese residents gave a check to the federal government to pay
for bombs to be used against the Japanese capital of Tokyo.
Six months later, General Emmons asked for 1,500 Nisei
volunteers for the army. More than 9,500 Nisei men of
Hawaii answered Emmons's call. Many of them were sent to
Camp Shelby, Mississippi, where they became members of the
442nd Regimental Combat Team. "I wanted to show something, to contribute to America," explained Minoru Hinahara,
who served as a Japanese language intepreter in the army's
27th Division. "My parents could not become citizens but
they told me, 'You fight for your country.'" He, and many
others, did exactly that.

With identification tags on their clothing and luggage, the Mochida family awaits removal to an American concentration camp.

Chapter Seven

The Internment

IN A SMALL JAPANESE FARMING COMMUNITY IN CALIFOR-
nia, Mary Tsukamoto was in church when she learned what
had happened far away in Hawaii. "I do remember Pearl
Harbor," she said years later as if it had happened that
morning. "It was a December Sunday, so we were getting ready
for our Christmas program. We were rehearsing and having
Sunday school class, and I always played the piano for the
adult Issei service. . . . After the service started, my husband
ran in. He had been home that day and heard [the an-
nouncement] on the radio. We just couldn't believe it, but he
told us that Japan attacked Pearl Harbor. I remember how
stunned we were. And suddenly the whole world turned dark."

Dark days indeed had arrived for Japanese on the
United States mainland, especially on the West Coast, where
most of them lived. Many of their fellow Americans turned
against the Japanese, fearing that their loyalties lay with Japan
rather than with the United States. Some voices, however,
urged fairness. The day after the attack on Pearl Harbor, one
congressman said, "It is my fervent hope and prayer that
residents of the United States of Japanese extraction will not
be made the victim of pogroms directed by self-proclaimed
patriots and by hysterical self-anointed heroes. . . . Let us not
make a mockery of our Bill of Rights by mistreating these
folks. Let us rather regard them with understanding, remem-
bering they are the victims of a Japanese war machine, with
the making of the international policies of which they had
nothing to do."

Even before the United States declared war on Japan,
the government had investigated the loyalty of Japanese in
America, both Issei (immigrants from Japan) and Nisei (Japanese Americans born in the United States). President

79

Roosevelt had secretly arranged to have a Chicago business-man named Curtis Munson gather information on Japanese Americans to see whether they were a threat to the nation's military security. Roosevelt received Munson's report on November 7, 1941, and asked the War Department to review it. Munson reported that there was no need to fear that America's Japanese population would be spies or saboteurs. He wrote, "There will be no armed uprising of Japanese [in this country]. . . . Japan will commit some sabotage largely depending on imported Japanese as they are afraid of and do not trust the Nisei. There will be no wholehearted response from Japanese in the United States. . . . For the most part the local Japanese are loyal to the United States or, at worst, hope that by remaining quiet they can avoid concentration camps or irresponsible mobs. We do not believe that they would be at least any more disloyal than any other racial group in the United States with whom we went to war."

Other government officials agreed with Munson that the Japanese in America posed no serious threat. Lieutenant Commander K. D. Ringle of the Office of Naval Intelligence investigated Japanese in Hawaii and on the mainland. He found that the large majority of them were loyal to the United States, and he estimated that only about 3,500 of them could possibly be considered military threats. He concluded that there was no need for mass action against the Japanese. The FBI had also made its own investigation. FBI Director J. Edgar Hoover arrested some people who were suspected of disloy-alty: 1,291 Japanese (367 in Hawaii, 924 on the mainland), 857 Germans, and 147 Italians. But Hoover felt that the nation's security did not require the mass internment of the Japanese.

Lieutenant General John L. DeWitt, head of the Western Defense Command (WDC), disagreed with these findings. DeWitt was the army officer in charge of military security in the western United States, and he believed the Japanese there were a threat. Among other things, he thought that they were sending radio messages to Japanese ships offshore. Soon after the attack on Pearl Harbor, DeWitt asked for permission to conduct search-and-seizure operations to shut down these supposed radio transmissions. The Justice Department decided that there was no evidence to issue search warrants, however, and the Federal Communications Commission, which had listened to all broadcasts, reported that DeWitt's fears were groundless.

Nevertheless, the army continued to assume that both Japanese immigrants and Japanese American citizens were

The confused, resentful people who were deposited in crowded assembly centers had no idea what their ultimate destination was to be.

disloyal. DeWitt asked for the power to keep them out of restricted areas. In early 1942, at a meeting of federal and state officials in his San Francisco headquarters, DeWitt said, "We are at war and this area—eight states—has been designated as a theater of operations. . . . [There are] approximately 288,000 enemy aliens . . . which we have to watch. . . . I have little confidence that the enemy aliens are law-abiding or loyal in any sense of the word. Some of them yes; many, no. Particularly the Japanese. I have no confidence in their loyalty

The Liberty Cafe in Boston betrayed its name with a sign declaring prejudice against people of Japanese descent.

whatsoever. I am speaking now of the native born Japanese—
117,000—and 42,000 in California alone."

Serving under DeWitt, Major General Joseph W.
Stilwell had an insider's view of the Western Defense Command. In his diary, Stilwell described DeWitt's irrational
reactions to rumors: "Common sense is thrown to the winds
and any absurdity is believed." Stilwell did not understand the
reasons for DeWitt's conduct, but Hoover, the head of the
FBI, saw what was really going on. Hoover knew that the
attitude of the WDC reflected "hysteria and lack of judg-
ment," yet he also realized that the proposal to take all
Japanese residents away from the coast and place them in
internment camps was a reaction to political and public
pressure, not to the facts. In short, powerful forces in government and among the American people wanted the Japanese to
be punished, whether or not they really were a military threat.

In the weeks right after Pearl Harbor, the newspapers
tended to be restrained. They told readers to remain calm and
considerate toward the Japanese. But soon the mood of the
media shifted. In January 1942, John B. Hughes of the Mutual
Broadcasting Company began a monthlong attack on the
Japanese in California. He charged that they were spies, and
that their success in growing produce was part of a master war
plan to control America's food supply. On January 19, *Time*
magazine wrote about Japanese espionage in Hawaii in an
article called "The Stranger Within Our Gates." The next day,
the San Diego *Union* stirred anti-Japanese hysteria with these
words: "In Hawaii . . . treachery by residents, who although
of Japanese ancestry had been regarded as loyal, has played an
important part in the success of Japanese attacks. . . . Every
Japanese . . . should be moved out of the coastal area and to

a point of safety far enough inland to nullify any inclination they may have to tamper with our safety here." And the *Los Angeles Times* said, "A viper is nonetheless a viper wherever the egg is hatched—so a Japanese American, born of Japanese parents—grows up to be a Japanese, not an American."

On January 29, a columnist for the Hearst chain of newspapers blasted the Japanese, saying, "I am for immediate removal of every Japanese on the West Coast to a point deep in the interior. I don't mean a nice part of the interior either. Herd 'em up, pack 'em off and give 'em the inside room in the badlands." Two weeks later, in the *Washington Post*, a well-known columnist named Walter Lippmann called for the mass removal of Japanese Americans. "The Pacific Coast is in imminent danger of a combined attack from within and without," he wrote. "The Pacific Coast is officially a combat zone. . . . And nobody ought to be on a battlefield who has no good reason for being there. There is plenty of room elsewhere for him to exercise his rights."

The press campaign for Japanese removal was joined by patriotic organizations. In January 1942 the American Legion of California began to demand that all Japanese who were citizens of both Japan and the United States should be placed in "concentration camps." American Legion groups in Washington State and Oregon passed resolutions urging that all Japanese be evacuated. In the January issue of their publication, the *Grizzly Bear,* the Native Sons and Daughters of the Golden West told their fellow Californians, "We told you so. Had the warnings been heeded—had the federal and state authorities been 'on the alert,' and rigidly enforced the Exclusion Law and the Alien Land Law . . . had the legislation been enacted denying citizenship to offspring of all aliens ineligible

to citizenship . . . had Japan been denied the privilege of using California as a breeding ground for dual-citizens (Nisei);—the treacherous Japs probably would not have attacked Pearl Harbor December 7, 1941, and this country would not today be at war with Japan."

The anti-Japanese chorus included voices from farming associations. "We've been charged with wanting to get rid of the Japs for selfish reasons," the Grower-Shipper Vegetable Association stated. "We might as well be honest. We do. It's a question of whether the white man lives on the Pacific Coast or the brown man. They came into this valley to work, and they stayed to take over. . . . If all the Japs were removed tomorrow, we'd never miss them in two weeks, because the white farmers can take over and produce everything the Jap grows."

The charges of widespread disloyalty among the Japanese were untrue, and so were claims that the attack on Pearl Harbor was somehow linked to the presence of a Japanese

A baseball game at the Manzanar camp.

85

population in America. Yet local and state politicians were already leading the movement for Japanese removal. Officials of 16 California counties, including Los Angeles County, urged the evacuation of the Japanese, as did the state's attorney general, who warned that the Japanese in California "may bring about a repetition of Pearl Harbor." Congressman Leland Ford of Los Angeles wrote to the War Department, the Navy, and the FBI, insisting that "all Japanese, whether citizens or not, be placed in concentration camps."

The situation on the West Coast was very different from that in Hawaii. Business leaders in Hawaii knew that the Japanese workers were a vital part of the islands' economy and did not want to lose them. Economic interests in California did not need Japanese labor, and many white farmers there viewed Japanese farmers as rivals. In Hawaii, Japanese made up a significant part of the total population. On the mainland, however, they were a tiny racial minority, vulnerable to prejudice and racist attacks.

By February of 1942, the army had made its position clear. DeWitt and other top officials formally requested permission to remove anyone who was suspected of being dangerous, whether that person was an immigrant or an American-born citizen. But the federal government still had not made a decision on the question of evacuation. During lunch with President Roosevelt on February 7, the nation's attorney general said "there were no reasons for mass evacuation." The secretary of war wrote in his diary that if the Japanese, especially those who were American citizens, were evacuated as a group solely because of their race, "it will make a tremendous hole in our constitutional system."

President Roosevelt was willing to make such a tremendous hole in the Constitution. In fact, he had been considering the internment of Japanese Americans for a long time. As early as 1936 he had suggested to a top navy officer that secret lists be drawn up of all Japanese in Hawaii who had any contact with Japanese ships calling in the islands. These people would be "the first to be placed in a concentration camp in the event of trouble." This document shows that five years before the attack on Pearl Harbor, Roosevelt was already making a plan to imprison Japanese residents in

The government put the interned Japanese to work. These internees are weeding onion fields at the Tule Lake camp in Northern California.

America in a "concentration camp" without any regard for their rights under the law.

On February 11, 1942, Roosevelt met with the secretary of war and gave his approval to the idea of evacuating Japanese from the West Coast. Three days later, General DeWitt sent the secretary his formal recommendation for interning the Japanese. His words show that racism, not military security, was the real reason for the internment. "The Japanese race is an enemy race," he wrote, "and while many second-and-third generation Japanese born on United States soil, possessed of United States citizenship, have become 'Americanized,' the racial strains are undiluted. . . . It, therefore, follows that along the vital Pacific Coast over 112,000 potential enemies, of Japanese extraction, are at large today."

A few days later, the attorney general of the United States tried one last time to argue that internment was unnecessary. He wrote to the president, saying, "My last advice from the War Department is that there is no evidence of imminent attack and from the FBI that there is no evidence of planned sabotage." But the voice of caution and law was drowned out by the shouts for evacuation. On February 19, President Roosevelt signed Executive Order 9066, which gave the secretary of war the power to determine who could enter or remain in any place that was considered a military area. In effect, the order gave the War Department complete control over the population of the West Coast.

Roosevelt's order did not identify the Japanese as the group to be taken out of the "military area." But the Japanese were unmistakably the target. A few months later, when President Roosevelt learned that the War Department was thinking about interning Germans and Italians on the East

Coast, he told the secretary of war to back off. Although the United States was at war with Germany and Italy as well as Japan, Germans and Italians in America were treated quite differently from Japanese there. Germans and Italians were white Europeans, but Japanese were "strangers from a different shore."

President Roosevelt had signed a blank check, giving full authority to General DeWitt to evacuate the Japanese and place them in internment camps. And so it happened, tragically for the Japanese and for the U.S. Constitution, for there was actually no military need for thousands of lives to be uprooted.

Under General DeWitt's command, the military posted orders for evacuation. They read: "Pursuant to the provisions of Civilian Exclusion Order No. 27, this Headquarters, dated April 30, 1942, all persons of Japanese ancestry, both alien and non-alien, will be evacuated from the above area by 12 o'clock noon, P.W.T., Thursday May 7, 1942." The evacuees were told to bring their bedding, toilet articles, extra clothing, and utensils—nothing more. "No pets of any kind will be permitted," said the order. Houses, furniture, cars, gardens, businesses—all must be left behind.

The Japanese stood silent and numb before the notices. Years later, Congressman Robert Matsui, who was a baby in 1942, asked, "How could I as a six-month-old child born in this country be declared by my own Government to be an enemy alien?" But the order applied to everyone, including children. An American birthright made absolutely no difference. "Doesn't my citizenship mean a single blessed thing to anyone?" asked one young Japanese American man in distress. Another recalled, "Several weeks before May, soldiers

Despite occasional games and pastimes, the camps were bleak and depressing places where families could not lead normal lives.

came around and posted notices on telephone poles. It was sad for me to leave the place where I had been living for such a long time. Staring at the ceiling in bed at night, I wondered who would take care of my cherry tree and my house after we moved out."

Notice of evacuation
One spring night
The image of my wife
Holding the hands of my mother.

Believing that the military orders were unconstitutional, Minoru Yasui of Portland, Oregon, refused to obey the military curfew, saying, "It was my belief that no military authority has the right to subject any United States citizen to any requirement that does not equally apply to all other U.S. citizens. If we believe in America, if we believe in equality and democracy, if we believe in law and justice, then each of us, when we see or believe errors are being made, has an obligation to make every effort to correct them."

Other Japanese also resisted. Fred Korematsu in California and Gordon Hirabayashi in Washington refused to report to the evacuation center. "As an American citizen," Hirabayashi explained, "I wanted to uphold the principles of the Constitution, and the curfew and evacuation orders which singled out a group on the basis of ethnicity violated them. It was not acceptable to me to be less than a full citizen in a white man's country." All three men were arrested, convicted, and sent to prison. They took their cases to the Supreme Court, which upheld their convictions, saying that the government's orders were based on military necessity.

Despite a few cases of resistance, most Japanese felt they had no choice but to obey the evacuation orders. Told that they could take only what they could carry, they had to sell most of their possessions. "I remember how agonizing was my despair," said Tom Hayase, "to be given only about six days in which to dispose of our property." Most had to sell their belongings for a fraction of what they were worth. One evacuee described the "feeling of despair and humiliation" felt by Japanese as the whites came and looked over their possessions, offering insultingly small sums. A few Japanese were able to leave their goods with non-Japanese friends, but most had no choice but to accept whatever they were offered. They did not know whether they would ever be able to come back; they did not know what the future held for them.

*A tearful mother and three children are evacuated from
their Washington State home to an uncertain future.*

Chapter Eight

"*Beyond the Barbed Wire Fence*"

THE EVACUATION ORDER AFFECTED 94,000 JAPANESE from California and 25,000 from Washington State and Oregon; more than half of them were U.S. citizens. As instructed by the posters that appeared on telephone poles and walls, the Japanese gathered at control centers, where they were registered. Each family was given a number. "Henry went to the Control Station to register the family," remembered Monica Sone. "He came home with twenty tags, all numbered '10710,' tags to be attached to each piece of baggage, and one to hang from our coat lapels. From then on, we were known as Family #10710." When they reported at the train stations, they found themselves surrounded by soldiers with rifles and bayonets.

> *Like a dog*
> *I am commanded*
> *At a bayonet point.*
> *My heart is inflamed*
> *With burning anguish.*

The evacuees were taken by train to assembly centers. "I looked at Santa Clara's streets from the train over the subway," wrote one man in a letter to friends in San Jose, California. "I thought this might be the last look at my loved home city. My heart almost broke, and suddenly hot tears just came pouring out." The evacuees knew that more than their homes and possessions had been taken from them. "On May 16, 1942, my mother, two sisters, niece, nephew, and I left . . . by train," said Teru Watanabe. "Father joined us later. Brother left earlier by bus. We took whatever we could carry. So much we left behind, but the most valuable thing I lost was my freedom."

When the trains reached their destinations, the evacuees were shocked to discover that they were to be housed at stockyards, fairgrounds, and racetracks. "The assembly center was filthy, smelly, and dirty," one remembered. "There were roughly two thousand people packed in one large building. No beds were provided, so they gave us gunny sacks to fill with straw, that was our bed." Stables served as housing: "Where a horse or cow had been kept, a Japanese American family was moved in." Another evacuee said, "Suddenly you realized that human beings were being put behind fences just like on the farm where we had horses and pigs in corrals."

> *If you live in a*
> *Horse stable*
> *The wind of cities*
> *Blows through.*

The assembly centers were crowded and noisy. "There was a constant buzzing—conversations, talk. Then, as the evening wore on, during the still of the night, things would get quiet, except for the occasional coughing, snoring, giggles. Then someone would get up to go to the bathroom. It was like a family of three thousand people camped out in a barn." Everywhere there were lines. An evacuee explained, "We lined up for mail, for checks, for meals, for showers, for washrooms, for laundry tubs, for toilets, for clinic service, for movies." There were curfews and roll calls, and "day and night camp police walked their beats within the center."

After a brief stay in the assembly centers, the evacuees were herded into 171 special trains, 500 people in each train. These trains would carry them to the internment camps where

they would live for an unknown period of time—for the duration of the war.

> Snow in mountain pass
> Unable to sleep
> The prison train.

The evacuees had no idea where they were going. In their pockets, some carried photographs of themselves and the homes they had left behind, and they occasionally turned their gaze away from the landscape whizzing by them and pulled out their pictures.

> Falling asleep with
> A photograph,
> Awakened by a dream,
> Cold snowy wind of
> Missoula.

The trains took them to 10 internment camps: Topaz in Utah; Poston and Gila River in Arizona; Amache in

Internees line up for inspection outside their hastily erected quarters.

95

Colorado; Jerome and Rohwer in Arkansas; Minidoka in Idaho; Manzanar and Tule Lake in California; and Heart Mountain in Wyoming.

Most of the camps were located in remote desert areas. "We did not know where we were," remembered an internee. "No houses were in sight, no trees or anything green—only scrubby sagebrush and an occasional low cactus, and mostly dry, baked earth." They looked around them and saw hundreds of miles of wasteland, "beyond the end of the horizon and again over the mountain—again, more wasteland." They were surrounded by dust and sand. At Minidoka, Monica Sone recalled, "we felt as if we were standing in a gigantic sand-mixing machine as the sixty-mile gale lifted the loose earth up into the sky, obliterating everything. Sand filled our mouths and nostrils and stung our faces and hands like a thousand darting needles."

In the camps, the internees were assigned to barracks. Each barrack measured about 20 by 120 feet and was divided into four or six rooms. Usually a family was housed in one room that measured 20 by 20 feet. One internee listed the usual furnishings of these rooms: "a pot bellied stove, a single electric light hanging from the ceiling, an Army cot for each person and a blanket for the bed."

> *Birds,*
> *Living in a cage,*
> *The human spirit.*

The camp was orderly and rigid. Barracks were lined up in straight rows; barbed wire fences with guard towers were the new borders of the internees' world. Some tried to make this harsh new environment more human by creating rock gardens with miniature trees outside their drab barracks.

The little gardens provided relief in a world of military-style routine. Recalled an internee, "Camp life was highly regimented and it was rushing to the wash basin to beat the other groups, rushing to the mess hall for breakfast, lunch and dinner." Every morning at 7:00 A.M., the internees were awakened by a siren blast. After eating breakfast in a cafeteria, the children went to school where they began the day by saluting the flag of the United States and then singing "My country, 'tis of thee, sweet land of liberty." Looking beyond the flagpole, they saw the barbed wire, the watchtowers, and the armed guards. "I was too young to understand," said George Takei years later, "but I remember soldiers carrying rifles, and I remember being afraid."

Most adults went to work. Shopkeepers and farmers suddenly found themselves working for the government as wage earners, forced to abandon the virtues of self-reliance and independence that had helped them survive in society. They worked as cooks, construction laborers, teachers, nurses, doctors, clerks, and unskilled workers, earning $12 a month as unskilled laborers, $16 as skilled, and $19 as professionals.

Busy and active before the evacuation, many internees became bored and listless:

> *Gazing at the barracks*
> *Where my wife exists,*
> *Beyond the barbed wire fence,*
> *I pluck and chew*
> *The leaves of grass.*

97

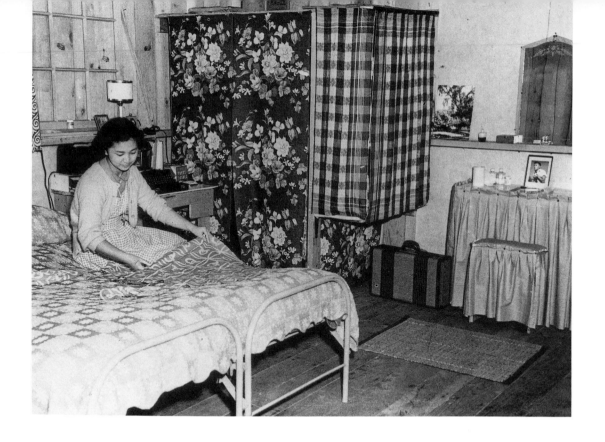

Many internees lost their homes, cars, and furniture. This woman and her husband furnished their room in a camp barracks with items made from scrap lumber.

They had been proud people before the evacuation, but now they felt smaller. Their dignity was destroyed. Some were overwhelmed by their despair.

> *A fellow prisoner*
> *Takes his life with poison.*
> *In the evening darkness,*
> *Streaks of black blood*
> *Stain the camp road.*

Family life was impossible in the camps. Families no longer sat down to eat together; instead, the internees ate at long tables in large mess halls. Parents often sat at separate tables from their children, especially the teenagers. People were "crowded in a long line just like a snake," waiting "for a meal in the dust and wind." Young married couples worried about having children born in the camps. "When I was

pregnant with my second child, that's when I flipped," said a
Nisei woman. "I guess that's when the reality really hit me. I
thought to myself, gosh, what am I doing getting pregnant. I
told my husband, 'This is crazy. You realize there's no future
for us and what are we having kids for?'"

But the war had also begun to open a future for the
Nisei. At first, all young Japanese men were classified as
enemy aliens. Even the Nisei, who had been born in the United
States and were U.S. citizens, were barred from serving in the
country's armed forces. In October 1942, however, the director of the Office of War Information (OWI) urged President
Roosevelt to allow Nisei to join the army and navy. "Loyal
American citizens of Japanese descent should be permitted,
after an individual test, to enlist in the Army and Navy," he
said. "This matter is of great interest to OWI. Japanese
propaganda to the Philippines, Burma, and elsewhere insists
that this is a racial war. We can combat this effectively with
counterpropaganda only if our deeds permit us to tell the
truth." In other words, Japan's accusation of racism in America would be weakened if America let U.S. citizens of Japanese
ancestry serve in the armed forces. Roosevelt understood this.
Although he had violated the civil rights of Japanese American
citizens by allowing them to be interned, he was willing to
protect their rights in another area if it were good public
relations to do so. On February 1, 1943, ignoring the evacuation order he had signed a year earlier, Roosevelt wrote, "No
loyal citizen of the United States should be denied the democratic right to exercise the responsibilities of his citizenship,
regardless of his ancestry. . . . Americanism is not, and never
was, a matter of race or ancestry. Every loyal American citizen

should be given the opportunity to serve this country . . . in the ranks of our armed forces."

Five days later the government required all internees to answer loyalty questionnaires. One of the purposes of the questionnaires was to register Nisei men in the camps for the military draft. Question 27 asked draft-age males, "Are you willing to serve in the armed forces of the United States on combat duty, wherever ordered?" Question 28 asked all internees, "Will you swear unqualified allegiance to the United States of America and faithfully defend the United States from any or all attack by foreign or domestic forces, and forswear any form of allegiance or obedience to the Japanese emperor, or any other foreign government, power, or organization?"

"I remember soldiers carrying rifles, and I remember being afraid," said George Takei *of* Star Trek *fame, recalling his childhood experience in an internment camp.*

Forced to fill out and sign the loyalty questionnaire, Nisei in the internment camps stared at the form:

> Loyalty, disloyalty,
> If asked,
> What should I answer?

Some 4,600 of the 21,000 draft-age Nisei males eligible to register for the draft gave no response or answered no to questions 27 and 28. Many of them said they were not expressing disloyalty but were protesting their internment. "Well, I am one of those that said 'no, no' on the questions, one of the 'no, no' boys," explained Albert Nakai, "and it is not that I was proud about it, it was just that our legal rights were violated and I wanted to fight back."

When he was told the army wanted Nisei to volunteer for a special combat unit, Dunks Oshima said, "What do they take us for? Saps?" He added that the government had a lot of nerve, after running him out of his hometown, to ask him "to volunteer for a suicide squad so I could get killed for this damn democracy."

At Heart Mountain internment camp, a Nisei named Frank Emi studied the questionnaire. "The more I looked at it the more disgusted I became," recalled Emi, who at the time was 27 years old with a wife and two children. "We were treated more like enemy aliens than American citizens." Emi posted his answer on the mess hall doors: "Under the present conditions and circumstances, I am unable to answer these questions." Shortly afterward, he attended a mass meeting where he heard a stirring speech by Kiyoshi Okamoto. An engineer from Hawaii who had moved to the mainland and become a high school teacher, Okamoto told his fellow Nisei that as American citizens they should stand up for the rights guaranteed to them under the Constitution. He referred to himself as the "Fair Play Committee of One." The 50-year-old Okamoto inspired the younger Nisei. "At first we were naive and just felt the questionnaire was unfair," said Emi. "But Okamoto taught us about the Constitution and it came to have great meaning as we began to resist."

Though most Nisei answered yes to questions 27 and 28, they did not rush to join the army. The army was able to recruit only 1,208 volunteers—a small percentage of those who were eligible to join. In January 1944, the army began drafting Nisei who had answered yes to the two questions. (People who enter the military by volunteering are recruits; those who are drafted are required by law to perform military service.) At Heart Mountain, Emi and several fellow Nisei organized the Fair Play Committee (FPC). They announced that they would resist the draft until their citizenship rights were restored. Their movement gathered widespread support. Four hundred Nisei attended their meetings. Draft resistance broke out in the other camps.

Worried, government authorities acted quickly to crush the protest. Emi and six other leaders of the Heart Mountain Fair Play Committee were arrested for conspiracy to resist the draft and for advising others to resist. James Omura, editor of the *Rocky Shimpo,* a Japanese newspaper in Denver, was arrested on the same charges because his paper had supported the Fair Play Committee. The cost of the trial bankrupted Omura's newspaper. Forty years later, though, he still defended his actions: "The *Shimpo* took up the cudgel of Nisei rights under the Constitution."

In court, Emi and the other leaders of the FPC argued that it was morally wrong and legally unconstitutional to draft Japanese Americans who had been interned in violation of their civil rights. "We, the members of the FPC, are not afraid to go to war—we are not afraid to risk our lives for our country," they had declared in their statement of resistance. "We would gladly sacrifice our lives to protect and uphold the principles and ideals of our country as set forth in the Constitution and the Bill of Rights, for on its inviolability depends the freedom, liberty, justice, and protection of all people including Japanese Americans and all other minority groups."

Emi and the others were found guilty and sentenced to four years at Leavenworth Federal Penitentiary. "What you guys are doing is all right," a Nisei told Emi. "But I don't want to go to jail so I have to register for the draft." At Leavenworth, Emi and his colleagues found themselves in a prison for hardened criminals. "They asked us, 'Why are you here?'" said Emi. "And we told them, and they replied, 'It don't make sense to put you in jail.'"

All in all, some 300 Nisei resisted the draft. Many of them were sent to prison. "Look, the government took my father away, and interned him someplace," explained a Nisei draft resister. "My mother is alone at the Grenada camp with my younger sister who is only fourteen." This young man felt it was wrong for the American government to treat him and his family as enemies and then ask him to fight for America. Such was the legacy of bitterness created by the internment camps.

Japanese American soldiers—here serving as interpreters in Burma—
helped the war effort in many ways.

Chapter Nine

Heroes
and
Homecomings

DURING WORLD WAR II, 33,000 JAPANESE AMERICANS served in the United States armed forces. They believed that helping to defend their country was the best way to show their loyalty and to fulfill their obligation as citizens. Several thousand of them were members of the Military Intelligence Service (MIS), working as interpreters and translators in the Pacific. Because they spoke Japanese, they were able to translate captured Japanese documents, including battle plans, lists of Imperial Navy ships, and Japanese secret codes. Their efforts often made the difference between victory and defeat. For example, Richard Sakakida's translation of Japanese plans for a landing on Bataan in the Philippines made it possible for American tanks to ambush the invaders as they landed.

Nisei soldiers also volunteered for service in Burma, in Southeast Asia. One of their officers described their heroic work: "During battles they crawled up close enough to be able to hear Jap officers' commands and to make verbal translations to our soldiers. They tapped lines, listened in on radios, translated documents and papers, made spot translations of messages and field orders."

Nisei soldiers took part in the invasion of Okinawa, a Japanese-held island group. Two of them, Hiroshi Kobashigawa and Frank Higashi, were worried about their families in Okinawa. Both of them had been born in the United States, but their parents had returned to Okinawa before the war started. When American soldiers landed in Okinawa, they found the people hiding in caves. The Japanese military had told the Okinawans that it would be better for them to be dead than to be captured by Americans, and the Okinawans were afraid they would be tortured, raped, and killed by the American soldiers. In his family's home village, Kobashigawa was relieved to find his mother, sister, and three younger brothers safe in a civilian refugee camp. Higashi found his father in the hills of northern Okinawa and carried him on his back to the village. Nisei soldiers like Kobashigawa and Higashi not only rescued their own families but also persuaded many Japanese soldiers to surrender. General Charles Willoughby, chief of intelligence in the Pacific, estimated that Nisei MIS contributions shortened the war by two years.

Nisei soldiers helped win the war in Europe, too. In 1942, while General DeWitt was shipping Japanese on the West Coast to the internment camps, General Emmons in Hawaii formed a combat battalion of Hawaiian Nisei. After training at Camp McCoy in Wisconsin and Camp Shelby in Mississippi, 1,400 Nisei of this battalion were sent to North Africa and then to Italy, where they helped the Allies conquer Italy. Three hundred of them were killed; 650 were wounded. They fought so bravely that they were called the "Purple Heart Battalion."

Nisei soldiers from Hawaii and from internment camps were formed into the 442nd Regimental Combat Team. The 442nd experienced bloody fighting in Italy. Then it was sent to France, where Nisei soldiers took the town of Bruyeres from German troops in heavy house-to-house fighting. After that, the 442nd was ordered to rescue the "Lost Battalion," 211 men from Texas surrounded by German troops in the Vosges Mountains of France. "If we advanced a hundred yards, that was a good day's job," recalled a Nisei soldier describing the rescue mission. "We'd dig in again, move up another hundred yards, and dig in. That's how we went. It took us a whole week to get to the Lost Battalion. It was just a tree-to-tree fight." At the end of the week of

fighting, they had suffered 800 casualties. When the trapped Texans finally saw the Nisei soldiers, some broke into sobs. One of the rescued soldiers remembered the moment: "[The Germans] would hit us from one flank and then the other, then from the front and the rear. . . . we were never so glad to see anyone as those fighting Japanese Americans."

Nisei soldiers went on to assault German troops on Mount Nebbione in Italy. "Come on, you guys, go for broke!" they shouted as they charged directly into the fire of enemy machine guns. Captain Daniel Inouye crawled to the flank of a gun post and pulled the pin on his grenade. "As I drew my arm back, all in a flash of light and dark I saw him, that faceless German," he remembered:

> And even as I cocked my arm to throw, he fired and his rifle grenade smashed into my right elbow and exploded and all but tore my arm off. I looked at it, stunned and unbelieving. It dangled there by a few

A Japanese American infantry unit crosses a bridge on the Italian front.

bloody shreds of tissue, my grenade still clenched in a fist that suddenly didn't belong to me any more. . . . I swung around to pry the grenade out of that dead fist with my left hand. Then I had it free and I turned to throw and the German was reloading his rifle. But this time I beat him. My grenade blew up in his face and I stumbled to my feet, closing on the bunker, firing my tommy gun left-handed, the useless right arm slapping red and wet against my side.

For the wounded Captain Inouye, the war was over. Two weeks later, in May 1945, the war in Europe came to an end for everyone. Nisei soldiers of the 442nd regiment had suffered 9,500 casualties, including 600 killed. "Just think of all those people—of the 990 that went over [with me], not

U.S. soldiers relax with a poker game after the Fifth Army's capture of Livorno, an Italian port.

more than 200 of them came back without getting hit," said 442nd veteran Shig Doi. "If you look at the 442nd boys, don't look at their faces, look at their bodies. They got hit hard, some lost their limbs." The 442nd, military observers agreed, was "probably the most decorated unit in United States military history." Its soldiers had earned 18,143 individual decorations, including a Congressional Medal of Honor, 47 Distinguished Service Crosses, 350 Silver Stars, 810 Bronze Stars, and more than 3,600 Purple Hearts. These Nisei had given their lives and limbs to prove their loyalty.

One of the Nisei soldiers explained the meaning of their sacrifice in a letter to a young Japanese woman in Hawaii, written from the European battlefront:

> My friends and my family—they mean everything to me. They are the most important reason why I am giving up my education and my happiness to go to fight a war that we never asked for. But our Country is involved in it. Not only that. By virtue of the Japanese attack on our nation, we as American citizens of Japanese ancestry have been mercilessly flogged with criticism and accusations. But I'm not going to take it sitting down! I may not be able to come back. But that matters little. My family and friends—they are the ones who will be able to back their arguments with facts. They are the ones who will be proud. In fact, it is better that we are sent to the front and that a few of us do not return, for the testimony will be stronger in favor of the folks back home.

"They bought an awful hunk of America with their blood," General Joseph Stilwell said of the Japanese American

Japanese American troops return to Hawaii after eighteen months of duty in Italy. The Japanese Americans were among the most decorated soldiers in the war.

soldiers. "You're damn right those Nisei boys have a place in the American heart, now and forever." After the war, Stilwell flew to California to award the Distinguished Service Cross to Kazuo Masuda. Sergeant Masuda of the 442nd had single-handedly fired a mortar on Nazi positions and had been killed at Cassino, Italy. On the porch of a frame shack in Orange County, Stilwell pinned the medal on Masuda's sister, Mary, who had just returned from one of the internment camps.

Several show-business figures took part in the ceremony. One of them was a young actor named Ronald Reagan, who paid tribute to the fallen Nisei soldier, saying, "Blood that has soaked into the sands of a beach is all of one color. America stands unique in the world, the only country not founded on race, but on a way—an ideal."

The Nisei soldiers had made an impact back home. A Filipino man told how his attitude toward Japanese Americans had been turned around by the heroism of the Nisei soldiers: "When Japan bombed Pearl Harbor, Manila, and all parts of the Philippines, I was entirely against the Japanese too. My feeling was 100% against them. But when those Japanese in the war showed their patriotism in favor of this country, I changed my mind. They should not have been taken [to internment camps]. Like the Italians and the Germans, all those born here are citizens. They should not have been suspected as spies."

On July 15, 1946, on the lawn of the White House, President Harry Truman welcomed home the Nisei soldiers of the 442nd. He told them, "You fought for the free nations of the world . . . you fought not only the enemy, you fought prejudice—and you won."

As they stood on the land of their birth, however, the Nisei were not sure they had defeated prejudice in America. Captain Inouye soon discovered that they had not won the war at home. He was on his way back to Hawaii in 1945 when he tried to get a haircut in San Francisco. Entering the barbershop with his empty right sleeve pinned to his army jacket covered with ribbons and medals for his military heroism, Inouye was told, "We don't serve Japs here." Another Nisei soldier from Hawaii reflected on the future of his fellow

Nisei from the mainland. He and his Hawaiian buddies would be returning to the islands to take up "again the threads of life" where they had been left off. But the mainland Nisei soldiers had "no home to return to except the wire-enclosed relocation centers."

Even before the end of the war, the evacuation order had been canceled, and the government had begun to close the internment camps. After giving the loyalty questionnaire to internees, government officials had let some of those who answered yes to questions 27 and 28 leave the camps, resettling them in cities like Denver, Salt Lake City, and Chicago. "I felt wonderful the day I left camp," recalled Helen Murao. "We took a bus to the railroad siding and then stopped somewhere to transfer, and I went in and bought a Coke, a nickel Coke. It wasn't the Coke, but what it represented—that I was free to buy it, that feeling was so intense."

After the war ended, would the internees be free to return to the West Coast and rebuild their communities? At a press conference in November of 1944, President Roosevelt was asked this question. In reply, he offered his vision of a Japanese population spread throughout the United States. He was not eager to see large numbers of internees returning to places like San Francisco and Los Angeles to form distinct Japanese American communities. Instead, he felt that Japanese families "scattered" through New York State, Georgia, and other parts of the country could "be worked into the community." After all, Roosevelt said, "they are American citizens, and they have certain privileges."

All of their rights guaranteed by the Constitution had been taken away, and now the Japanese were being told they were American citizens and had "certain privileges." At last they could leave the internment camps—but the president wanted them scattered, for they should not be permitted to make other Americans uncomfortable. "My parents did not know what to do or where to go after they had been let out of camp," said Aiko Mifune. Her mother, Fusayo Fukuda Kaya, had come to America in 1919; she and her husband Yokichi had been tenant farmers in California before they were interned in Poston, Arizona. "But everything they had worked for was gone," explained Mifune. "They seemed listless and they stayed in Arizona and tried to grow potatoes there."

Despite the president's wishes, most of the newly freed internees wanted to go home to the West Coast. They boarded trains bound for Los Angeles, Seattle, and San Francisco. When a group of returning Japanese stepped from the

A Japanese American woman receives the Congressional Medal of Honor for her son, Sadao Munemori, who was killed when he threw himself on a hand grenade in Italy to save the lives of his fellow soldiers.

Daniel Inouye, who lost an arm in Italy, was the first Japanese American to serve in the U.S. Congress.

train in San Jose, they were welcomed home by some black and white women, who gave them hot food and then drove them to their places of lodging. But often, at other train stations, returning internees were met with hostile signs: No Japs Allowed, No Japs Welcome. When they finally saw their homes again, many found their houses damaged and their fields ruined.

An uncertain, fearful future seemed to await all of those who returned from the camps. They had suffered years of disgrace and anger that they would never forget. Some of them never were able to return home: too old, too ill, or too brokenhearted, they died in camp. Tragically, they had come all the way to America only to be buried in the forlorn and windswept cemeteries of desert camps. Their dreams did not deserve such an ending.

When the war is over
And after we are gone

Who will visit
This lonely grave in the wild
Where my friend lies buried?

To confront the problem of racism today, Asian Americans know they must remember the past and correct the injustice of internment. This need was felt deeply by Japanese Americans in the 1980s, when a government commission was deciding whether Japanese Americans should be paid compensation for their losses and suffering during the World War II internment.

The internment nightmare has haunted the older generation like ghosts. For years, the former prisoners felt unable to speak out and express their anger.

When we were children,
you spoke Japanese
in lowered voices
between yourselves.

Once you uttered secrets
which we should not know,
were not to be heard by us.
When you spoke
of some dark secret
You would admonish us,
"Don't tell it to anyone else."
It was a suffocated vow of silence.

The former internees have been carrying the "burden of shame" for half a century. "They felt like a rape victim," explained Congressman Norman Mineta, who had been in-

*Fred Korematsu, Minoru
Yasui, and Gordon
Hirabayashi (left to right)
went to court in 1983 to
challenge past Supreme Court
rulings that had allowed the
internment of Japanese Americans during World War II.*

terned at the Heart Mountain camp. "They were accused of
being disloyal. They were the victims but they were on trial
and they did not want to talk about it."

But *Sansei*, third-generation Japanese Americans, want
their elders to tell their story. Warren Furutani, for example,
told the commissioners that young people like himself had
been asking their parents to tell them about the concentration
camps and to join them in pilgrimages to the internment camp
at Manzanar. "Why? Why!" their parents would reply defen-
sively. "Why would you want to know about it? It's not
important, we don't need to talk about it." Furutani explained
that the former internees need to tell the world what happened
during those painful years.

Suddenly, during the commission hearings, scores of Issei and Nisei came forward and told their stories. "For over thirty-five years I have been the stereotype Japanese American," Alice Tanabe Nehira told the commission. "I've kept quiet, hoping in due time we will be justly compensated and recognized for our years of patient effort. By my passive attitude, I can reflect on my past years to conclude that it doesn't pay to remain silent."

The act of speaking out allowed the Japanese American community to unburden itself of years of anger and anguish. Sometimes the testimonies before the commission were long. The speakers were urged to finish. But they insisted the time was theirs. "Mr. Commissioner," protested poet Janice Mirikitani,

> *So when you tell me my time is*
> *up I tell you this.*
> *Pride has kept my lips*
> *pinned by nails,*
> *my rage coffined.*
> *But I exhume my past*
> *to claim this time.*

The former internees had finally spoken, and their voices compelled the nation do something to make up for the injustice of internment. In August 1988, Congress passed a bill giving an apology and a payment of $20,000 to each survivor of the internment camps. When President Ronald Reagan signed the bill into law, he admitted that the United States had committed "a grave wrong." During World War II, he said, Japanese Americans had remained "utterly loyal" to the United States. "Indeed, scores of Japanese Americans volunteered for our armed forces—many stepping forward in the internment camps themselves," Reagan declared. "The 442nd Regimental Combat Team, made up entirely of Japanese Americans, served with immense distinction—to defend this nation, their nation. Yet, back at home, the soldiers' families were being denied the very freedom for which so many of the soldiers themselves were laying down their lives."

The president then recalled something that had happened 43 years earlier. At a ceremony to award the Distinguished Service Cross to Kazuo Masuda, who had been killed in action and whose family had been interned, a young actor paid tribute to the slain Nisei soldier. That actor was Ronald Reagan. Now, as president, he apologized for the internment. The time had come, the president said, to end "a sad chapter in American history."

Chronology

1836	The first Chinese are employed as plantation workers in Hawaii.
1849	The California gold rush begins; Chinese immigrants are among the "Forty-Niners" who flock to California to seek their fortunes.
1868	A period of rapid modernization begins in Japan; Japan's military strength begins to grow.
1875	Congress limits the entry of Chinese women into the United States.
1882	The Chinese Exclusion Act is passed to keep Chinese laborers out of the United States.
1886	Large-scale immigration of Japanese into Hawaii begins.
1888	The first Japanese laborers are brought to California.
1890s	Large-scale immigration of Japanese into the United States begins.
1898	The United States takes possession of Hawaii and the Philippine Islands.
1900	Hawaii becomes a territory of the United States.
1903	Koreans begin emigrating to Hawaii and the U.S. mainland.

1904	Japanese troops invade Korea.
1906	Filipino immigration into Hawaii begins.
1907	Workers from India begin emigrating to the United States.
1908	Japan agrees to limit the number of Japanese who can go to the United States.
1910	Japan claims possession of Korea.
1920	Large-scale Filipino immigration into the U.S. mainland begins.
1921	Japan ends the practice of sending picture brides to the United States.
1924	Congress passes an immigration law that prevents Asians from immigrating into the United States.
1931	Japan invades Manchuria, a region in northeastern China, launching a campaign of aggression throughout Asia and the Pacific Islands.
1937	Full-scale war breaks out in China between Japanese and Chinese forces.
1939	Germany invades Poland; the war begins in Europe, with Great Britain and France allied against Germany and Italy.
1941	Japan bombs the U.S. naval base at Pearl Harbor, Hawaii, on December 7; the United States declares war on Japan and enters the war in Europe.
1942	President Roosevelt authorizes the internment of West Coast residents of Japanese descent.
1943	The U.S. Congress allows limited immigration from China and permits Chinese immigrants to become naturalized citizens.
1945	The war in Europe ends with the surrender of Germany in May; the United States drops two

atomic bombs on Japan in August; Japan surrenders.

1946   The Philippines become an independent nation; Congress allows limited immigration from India and permits Indian immigrants to become naturalized citizens.

1959   Hawaii is granted U.S. statehood.

1988   Congress passes a bill apologizing for the internment of Japanese Americans during World War II and providing compensation for the survivors.

Further Reading

Allen, Peter. *The Origins of World War II.* New York: Watts, 1992.

Buaken, Manuel. *I Have Lived with the American People.* Caldwell, ID: Caxton, 1948.

Bulosan, Carlos. *America is in the Heart: A Personal History.* 1946. Reprint. Seattle: University of Washington Press, 1981.

Charyn, Jerome. *Back to Bataan.* New York: Farrar, Straus & Giroux, 1993.

Choy, Bong-Yuon. *Koreans in America.* Chicago: Nelson-Hall, 1979.

Daley, William. *The Chinese Americans.* New York: Chelsea House, 1987.

Daniels, Roger. *Prisoners Without Trial: Japanese Americans in World War II.* New York: Hill & Wang, 1993.

Daniels, Roger, ed. *Japanese Americans: From Relocation to Redress.* Seattle: University of Washington Press, 1992.

Dower, John W. *War Without Mercy: Race and Power in the Pacific War.* New York: Pantheon, 1986.

Hamanaha, Sheila. *The Journey: Japanese Americans, Racism, and Renewal.* New York: Watts, 1990.

Higa, Karin, ed. *The View from Within: Japanese American Art from the Internment Camps, 1942–1945.* Los Angeles:

University of California at Los Angeles Asian American
Studies Center, 1992.

Kitano, Harry. *The Japanese Americans.* New York: Chelsea
House, 1988.

Knaefler, Tomi K. *Our House Divided: Seven Japanese American
Families in World War II.* Honolulu: University of Hawaii
Press, 1991.

Lehrer, Brian. *The Korean Americans.* New York: Chelsea House,
1988.

Melendy, H. Brett. *Asians in America: Filipinos, Koreans, and East
Indians.* Boston: Twayne, 1977.

Stern, Jennifer. *The Filipino Americans.* New York: Chelsea
House, 1989.

Tajiri, Vincent, ed. *Through Innocent Eyes: Teen-Agers' Impression
of World War II Internment Camp Life.* Los Angeles: Keiro
Services, 1990.

Tateishi, John. *And Justice for All: An Oral History of the Japanese
American Detention Camps.* New York: Random House,
1984.

TenBroek, Jacobus, et al. *Prejudice, War and the Constitution:
Causes and Consequences of the Evacuation of the Japanese Americans in World War II.* Berkeley and Los Angeles: University
of California Press, 1970.

Index

PICTURE CREDITS

RONALD TAKAKI, the son of immigrant plantation laborers from Japan, graduated from the College of Wooster, Ohio, and earned his Ph.D. in history from the University of California at Berkeley, where he has served both as the chairperson and the graduate adviser of the Ethnic Studies program. Professor Takaki has lectured widely on issues relating to ethnic studies and multiculturalism in the United States, Japan, and the former Soviet Union and has won several important awards for his teaching efforts. He is the author of six books, including the highly acclaimed *Strangers from a Different Shore: A History of Asian Americans*, and the recently published *A Different Mirror: A History of Multicultural America*.

REBECCA STEFOFF is a writer and editor who has published more than 50 nonfiction books for young adults. Many of her books deal with geography and exploration, including the three-volume set *Extraordinary Explorers*, recently published by Oxford University Press. Stefoff also takes an active interest in environmental issues. She served as editorial director for two Chelsea House series—*Peoples and Places of the World* and *Let's Discover Canada.* Stefoff studied English at the University of Pennsylvania, where she taught for three years. She lives in Portland, Oregon.

1996   22
last circ 2008

yel